Fresh Ideas Series

ILLUSTRATIONS STORIES AND QUOTES

to Hang Your Message On

Jim Burns and Greg McKinnon

(General Editor)   (Compiler)

Gospel Light

Gospel Light is an evangelical Christian publisher dedicated to serving the local church. We believe God's vision for Gospel Light is to provide church leaders with biblical, user-friendly materials that will help them evangelize, disciple and minister to children, youth and families.

We hope this Gospel Light resource will help you discover biblical truth for your own life and help you minister to youth. God bless you in your work.

For a free catalog of resources from Gospel Light please contact your Christian supplier or call 1-800-4-GOSPEL.

PUBLISHING STAFF
William T. Greig, Publisher
Dr. Elmer L. Towns, Senior Consulting Publisher
Dr. Gary S. Greig, Senior Consulting Editor
Jill Honodel, Editor
Pam Weston, Assistant Editor
Kyle Duncan, Associate Publisher
Bayard Taylor, M.Div., Editor, Theological and Biblical Issues
Debi Thayer, Designer

ISBN 0-8307-1883-4
© 1997 by Jim Burns
All rights reserved.
Printed in U.S.A.

Contents

Illustrations and Stories

God's Gifts to Us

Christ's Sacrifice

Victory over Sin and Death

God's Love

God's Presence Through Difficulties

God's Power and Strength

God's Powerful Word

God's Grace

Abundant Life

Contents

Our Relationship with God

Making Choices

Obedience

Commitment

Contentment

Faith

Suffering

Contents

Our Relationships with Others

Contents

Quotes

Dedication

This book is dedicated...

to my wife Hope,
who for the past 19 years has been a
living illustration of God's love to me.

to my son Wesley,
who can *tell* stories with the best of them.

and to my daughter Faith,
who says many things every day worth *quoting.*

Greg McKinnon
Auburn, Alabama

Contributors

Acknowledgments

Wally Coots

Minister to Students,
Forest Park Covenant Church, Muskegon, Michigan
24-year youth ministry veteran

Mike DeVries

High School Pastor,
Yorba Linda Friends Church, Yorba Linda, California
NIYM associate and author of the YouthBuilders Group
Bible Study Series *The Word on the New Testament*

Joel Lusz

Family Life Pastor,
Palm Beach Community Church,
Palm Beach Gardens, Florida
15-year youth ministry veteran

Dave Mahoney

Youth Pastor,
Fellowship Bible Church, Little Rock, Arkansas
21-year youth ministry veteran

Greg McKinnon

Director of Youth Ministries,
Auburn United Methodist Church, Auburn, Alabama
22-year youth ministry veteran

Eddie Willis

Director of Youth Ministries,
First United Methodist Church, Starksville, Mississippi
8 years experience in youth ministry

Chuck Wysong

Director of Youth Ministries for the Evangelical Covenant
Church
Teaches youth ministry at North Park College and
Seminary, Chicago, Illinois
18-year youth ministry veteran

Illustrations and Stories

Introduction

An illustration is a "picture taken with words." There is almost nothing more powerful than a story that makes a point. How interesting that as children we were often raised on stories. We cuddled up on a family member's lap and listened to a story we had heard a hundred times before, but nevertheless we wanted to hear it again! Illustrations paint a picture in our minds, and some of the best stories we have heard over the years actually become living pictures inside us.

The Master Teacher, Jesus Christ, often illustrated His points with stories and parables. He understood that our minds will often learn best from a powerful story. Jesus used common everyday illustrations that people of His day could easily understand. He had the ability to say, "Here's My point; now let Me illustrate that point for you." And He did it in a way that we can never forget it.

The great communicators of our day use the same method to get their message across to their audiences just as Jesus did so effectively almost 2000 years ago. For a moment think of the most influential communicators in your life and I'm sure you will agree that they have an incredible ability to illustrate truth to you through an appropriate story.

As a youth and family worker, one of my main jobs is to plant the Word of God in the lives of the young people I have the privilege to speak to. There is not a day that goes by in which I am not looking for one more illustration that will be appropriate for my message to kids and their families. Some of my favorite illustrations and quotes have been included in this book. I have also found new ones that I think are "out-of-the-park home runs."

In this volume, my good friend and longtime fellow youth worker, Greg McKinnon, has collected some of the finest illustrations I have ever seen or heard. The applications and Scriptures work. I know—I've already used some of them!

I have no doubt that this volume of illustrations and quotes will become one of your most often used resources to help kids and their families get the picture and visualize the Word. Thank you for all you do to make a difference in the lives of families who desperately need the hope you offer. When I was a brand new Christian, my youth worker, John Watson, one night gave us an illustration about God giving each one of us our parents. Today (26 years later) I have used that same illustration to illuminate the point I wanted to make to a group of students. Who is to say that one of the illustrations or quotes from this book will not be the life-changing point that one of your students will hold on to and then pass on to another generation?

Yours in Christ,

Jim Burns, Ph.D.
President, National Institute of Youth Ministry
San Clemente, California

God's Gifts to Us

Christ's Sacrifice

Martin and Morgan

KEY VERSES

"For Christ's love compels us, because we are convinced that one died for all, and therefore all died. And he died for all, that those who live should no longer live for themselves but for him who died for them and was raised again."
2 Corinthians 5:14,15

Once there were two identical twins named Martin and Morgan. They looked so alike that even their closest friends could not tell them apart by their looks. But looks was the *only* way they were alike. They certainly didn't act alike. Martin was the perfect child. He always obeyed his parents; he was kind to other people; he studied hard in school; and he had high moral standards and values.

Morgan, on the other hand, was a different story. He was constantly being disobedient to his parents; he mistreated other kids; he lied; he took things that didn't belong to him; and he was always in trouble. He was continually breaking his parents' hearts.

As Martin and Morgan grew older, the differences between them also grew. Martin continued to be the model student, applying himself and excelling in everything he did.

Morgan, however, got into deeper and deeper trouble. He began to have run-ins with the law. First it was for minor offenses like traffic violations and truancy. But the older he got the more serious the trouble became. He was in and out of jail as a teenager, then as a young adult he committed the ultimate crime. He killed someone and was found guilty of first-degree murder and was sentenced to die in the electric chair. He was placed on death row. Finally, he exhausted all the appeals and the execution date was set.

The day before he was to die, Martin came to visit him on death row. The guard opened Morgan's cell and let Martin in and then walked away. Immediately Martin began taking off his clothes and told Morgan to do the same. Martin then put on Morgan's clothes and had Morgan put on his. A few minutes later the guard came back to let Martin out of the cell, but instead it was Morgan who walked out, down the hall and out the door to freedom.

The next day they came to take Morgan to the electric chair, without realizing he was actually Martin. They walked him down the hall to the electric chair, strapped him in and ended his life.

Morgan was free, but he had a decision to make. He could either continue to live his life like he had always lived it—chances were he would be discovered and end up back on death row. Or he could take on Martin's lifestyle and try to imitate his life.

Christ willingly took your place on the cross. Now you have a decision to make: Will you live for Him or continue to live for yourself?

John 10:1-18; 15:13; Romans 4:25; 5:6-8;
1 Peter 2:21-24; 3:18; 1 John 3:16; 4:10

The Great Decision

KEY VERSE

"'Greater love has no one than this, that he lay down his life for his friends.'" John 15:13

Very early in the twentieth century a little boy was told by his doctor that he could save his sister's life by giving her some blood. The six-year-old girl was near death, the victim of a disease from which the boy had recovered two years earlier. Her only chance for survival was a blood transfusion from someone who had previously overcome the illness. Since the two children had the same rare blood type, the boy was the ideal donor.

"Johnny, would you like to give blood for Mary?" the doctor asked.

The boy hesitated. His lower lip started to tremble. Then he smiled and said, "Sure Doc. I'll give my blood for my sister."

Soon the two children were wheeled into the operating room—Mary was pale and thin; Johnny was the picture of health. Neither spoke, but when their eyes met, Johnny grinned.

As his blood siphoned into Mary's veins, you could almost see new life come into her tired body. The ordeal was almost over when Johnny's brave little voice broke the silence. "Say Doc, when do I die?"

It was only then that the doctor realized what the moment of hesitation, the trembling of the lip, had meant earlier. Little Johnny actually thought that in giving his blood to his sister he was giving up his life! And in that brief moment, he made the great decision!

God's Gifts to Us

Christ's Sacrifice

APPLICATION

Jesus loved you so much that He willingly laid down His life for you. Be willing to love other people just as Christ loves you.

ADDITIONAL SCRIPTURES

Luke 14:28; John 3:16; 10:11; Romans 5:6-8; Ephesians 5:1,2; 1 Peter 3:18; 1 John 3:16

Twice God's

> "'For even the Son of Man did not come to be served, but to serve, and to give his life a ransom for many.'"
> Mark 10:45

There was a little boy one time who loved boats, and he was also very handy with his hands. So one day he decided that he was going to make himself a boat. He began working on it every spare minute he had. When he finished, it was perfect in every detail.

The little boy's favorite pastime was sailing his handmade boat. He would take it down to the large lake near his house and sail it along the shore.

One day while he was sailing, the wind began to pick up. He ran to get the boat before the wind pushed it too far out, but he was too late. He pulled off his shoes and waded out into the water, but he still couldn't reach it, and the wind was getting stronger and stronger. He ran back to his house to get his father to help. His father went back with him, but the boat was nowhere in sight. The little boy went home with his father, heartbroken.

All the little boy seemed to do after that was mope around. One day he was walking slowly home from school when he glanced up into a pawnshop window and there was his boat. He ran into the pawnshop shouting, "That's my boat, that's my boat!"

The owner of the pawnshop looked at him and said, "No, that's my boat, if you want it you'll have to buy it."

The boy looked at the price tag and it was extremely high, because it was such a great little boat. He didn't know what to do so he went home and began to think of ways to raise money.

He picked up odd jobs around the neighborhood cutting grass, raking leaves, washing cars and anything else anyone would hire him to do. Each week he would count his money.

Finally after several weeks he had earned enough money to buy the little boat. So he took his piggy bank and ran all the way to the pawnshop. He ran into the shop and put the bank down on the counter so hard that it broke open. He told the pawnshop owner that he had come to buy his boat. The owner counted the money, to make sure it was all there, then he went over to the shelf, got the boat and handed it to the little boy. The shop owner heard the little boy say, as he walked out the door, "Little boat, you're twice mine. First I made you and now I bought you."

APPLICATION

You are twice God's. First He made you, then through the death of His Son He bought you. Live for Him out of gratitude for all He has done for you.

ADDITIONAL SCRIPTURES

Matthew 13:45,46; 18:12-14; 20:28; Luke 15:4-24; 19:10; Acts 20:28; 1 Corinthians 6:20; 1 Timothy 2:1-6; Hebrews 9:11-15

Big Jim Took His Place

KEY VERSE

"He himself bore our sins in his body on the tree, so that we might die to sins and live for righteousness; by his wounds you have been healed." 1 Peter 2:24

In a mountain community there was once a one-room school where the kids were so bad that they could never keep a teacher. Teachers usually only lasted a few weeks before they would give up and leave. Finally a new teacher came who really seemed to be different. The first thing he did was tell the class that he was doing away with all the rules and was going to let them make up their own rules as well as the penalties for breaking the rules.

They began making the rules and Big Jim, the largest boy in the class, stood up and said, "There needs to be a rule against taking someone's lunch and the penalty should be four licks across the back with the leather strap."

The teacher wrote down Big Jim's rule as well as all the other rules that were made.

One day after lunch Big Jim stood up and said, "Someone took my lunch."

The teacher began to ask questions and found out that Billy, a thin, undernourished boy, whose family was among the poorest of the poor, had taken the lunch. The teacher brought Billy to the front of the room, made him take off his shirt and lean over the desk for his whipping. His ribs poked out of his thin frail body. The teacher raised the leather strap and was ready to bring it down on Billy's trembling back when all of a sudden he heard Big Jim's husky voice shout, "Hold it, teacher!" as he came walking to the front of the room, taking off his shirt as he came.

"Let me take his whoop'n for 'im," he begged, as he lean-ed over Billy.

   The teacher didn't know what to say, but knowing that the penalty had to be paid, he consented and laid the leather strap to the back of Big Jim with such force that even Jim winced and his eyes watered. Billy never forgot the day that Big Jim took his place.

Christ took your punishment. He paid the debt for your sin because you couldn't.

Isaiah 53:4-12; Ephesians 2:8,9; Colossians 2:13-15; Hebrews 9:26-28; 1 Peter 3:18

The Knitting Needle

KEY VERSE

"He was pierced for our transgressions, he was crushed for our iniquities; the punishment that brought us peace was upon him, and by his wounds we are healed." Isaiah 53:5

There was once a young boy named Jim whose parents died when he was very young. His grandmother took him in, and by herself, tried to raise him. She was old and had very little money, but she loved him and worked long, hard hours to provide for him.

One day when little Jim came home from school his grandmother discovered that he had some things that didn't belong to him. He had stolen them from some of his classmates. His grandmother told him that it was wrong to take something that didn't belong to him even if other people had more than he did. She made him promise never to steal anymore. He promised, but it was not long before he broke his promise and his grandmother found out.

She asked Jim to come with her and she turned and walked down the hall of their small house toward the kitchen. On the way she stopped and took a knitting needle from her knitting bag. When they got to the kitchen she turned on one of the burners on the gas stove and laid the knitting needle across the hot flames. Jim watched as the knitting needle got hotter and hotter until finally it was red hot.

His grandmother then picked up the needle with a pot holder and held it up where little Jim could see its sizzling hot metal. Then she told Jim, "If I ever catch you stealing

anything again, I'm going to put this red hot knitting needle in the palm of your hand. Little Jim's eyes were as big as saucers and he was so scared that he promised her he would never steal again.

But as time passed Jim's fear of the knitting needle faded and he began to steal again. Finally he was caught by his grandmother. She confronted him and asked him to come with her. They started walking down the hall toward the kitchen and on the way she picked up the knitting needle. Jim was so afraid he began to shake. His grandmother grabbed his hand and pulled him down the hall toward the kitchen.

Once in the kitchen she turned on the burner and laid the knitting needle across the flame. Little Jim shook with fear and began to cry as he saw the needle getting hotter and hotter. His grandmother held his little hand tight. She then picked up the needle with the pot holder, stretched open Jim's palm and brought down the needle. But at the last moment she let go of Jim's hand and put the needle in her own.

After that day, Jim never stole anything again. What fear could not do, the sacrificial love of his grandmother did.

You should want to obey God, not out of fear of what might happen to you if you don't, but out of love for the One who first loved you.

Isaiah 53; Romans 8:1,2; Ephesians 2:1-9; Philippians 2:6-8; Hebrews 9:28; 1 Peter 2:24; 3:18

God's Gifts to Us

Christ's Sacrifice

Stained by the Blood

KEY VERSE

"How much more, then, will the blood of Christ, who through the eternal Spirit offered himself unblemished to God, cleanse our conscience from acts that lead to death, so that we may serve the living God!" Hebrews 9:14

Allen Walker, a great Australian preacher, shared the following story of something he observed.

As he was driving back to Sydney late one afternoon through the beautiful rolling hills, he looked up and saw a large hawk circling above. As he traveled around the bend, he lost sight of the big hawk. Then he turned a bend and saw a herd of sheep. He noticed that one little sheep was isolated, and the hawk was attacking this one isolated sheep. Walker parked his car and ran out into the field. When he reached down to get the sheep, it fell over. It was then he noticed that under her was a little newborn lamb. The little lamb was alive, yet stained by its mother's blood.

APPLICATION

On calvary the Savior took your punishment upon Himself, covering your sins with His blood and saving you from eternal death.

Christ's Sacrifice

_____

Isaiah 53:4-7; Mark 14:23,24; John 10:11-18;
Hebrews 9:12-14; 1 Peter 2:23-25

Rescued

KEY VERSE

"God demonstrates his own love for us in this: While we were still sinners, Christ died for us."
Romans 5:8

A little girl whose parents had died lived with her grandmother and slept in an upstairs bedroom. One night there was a fire in the house. The fire spread quickly and the first floor of the house was soon engulfed in flames. The grandmother perished while trying to rescue the child.

Neighbors called the fire department, then stood helplessly by, unable to enter the house because flames blocked all the entrances. The little girl appeared at an upstairs window, crying for help, just as word spread among the crowd that the firefighters would be delayed a few minutes because they were at another fire.

Suddenly, a man appeared with a ladder, put it up against the side of the house and disappeared inside. When he reappeared, he had the little girl in his arms. He delivered the child to the waiting arms below, then disappeared into the night. An investigation revealed that the child had no living relatives, and weeks later a meeting was held in the town hall to determine who would take the child into their home and bring her up.

A teacher said she would like to raise the child. She pointed out that she could ensure a good education. A farmer pointed out that living on a farm was healthy and satisfying. Others spoke, giving their reasons why it was to the child's advantage to live with them.

Finally, the town's richest resident arose and said, "I can give this child all the advantages that you have mentioned here, plus money and everything that money can buy."

Throughout all this, the child remained silent, her eyes on the floor.

"Does anyone else want to speak?" asked the chairperson. A man came forward from the back of the hall. His gait was slow and he seemed in pain. When he got to the front of the room, he stood directly before the little girl and held out his arms. The crowd gasped. His hands and arms were terribly scarred.

The child cried out, "This is the man who rescued me!" With a leap, she threw her arms around the man's neck, holding on for dear life, just as she had that fateful night. She buried her face in his shoulder and sobbed for a few moments. Then she looked up and smiled at him.

"This meeting is adjourned," said the chairperson.

APPLICATION

Jesus did not merely *tell* you He loves you, but He *proved* His love for you by His actions.

ADDITIONAL SCRIPTURES

Matthew 27:45-56; John 3:16; 15:13; 1 Peter 2:21-24; 3:18; 4:1

Free, but Still Locked Up

KEY VERSE

"So if the Son sets you free, you will be
free indeed." John 8:36

The great Houdini, being a master magician and a great locksmith, once bragged that there wasn't a jail cell in the world he couldn't escape from, provided he could go into the cell dressed in his street clothes and work in complete privacy.

A small town in England had built a new jail, which they believed was escape-proof, so they invited Houdini to come and try to break out. Houdini accepted the challenge. They put him in the cell and closed the door. He was left alone.

He took off his belt and took from it a tough, flexible steel rod. He went to work on the lock. He worked longer than it had ever taken him before and he still couldn't get the lock open! As time passed, he was becoming exhausted. He was stumped!

Finally, after two solid hours of work, Houdini collapsed from exhaustion. He fell against the door to the cell, and when he did the door swung open! It had been unlocked all the time.

_____ **APPLICATION**

You cannot overcome sin in your life by your own effort
and hard work, but when you admit that you are helpless
and turn to God, He'll set you free.

_____ **ADDITIONAL SCRIPTURES**

Isaiah 61:1 (also Luke 4:18,21); John 8:31-36;
Romans 6:16-18,22; 8:1,2; 2 Corinthians 3:17;
Galatians 5:1

God's Gifts to Us

Victory over
Sin and Death

Trying to Stop Death

KEY VERSES

"Since the children have flesh and blood, he too
shared in their humanity so that by his death he
might destroy him who holds the power of death—
that is, the devil—and free those who all their lives
were held in slavery by their fear of death."
Hebrews 2:14,15

Dr. Pierce Harris told the story about a dear Christian
woman who became very weak. She went to her physician, and he administered a series of tests and told her
she had cancer. With compassion, the physician told her
that her condition was not good. He shared with her that
she had a type of cancer that was very rare, but it was also
a rapidly spreading type. She asked the doctor, "How
long do I have?"

He responded, "You have at the outset three months to
live."

When she returned home, her pastor came to see her.
After telling him the news, he asked her, "How are you
doing?"

She said, "I'm fine, but I am having difficulty telling my
little boy, Billy. Five times I've tried to tell him, and I just
can't do it. Will you please tell him for me?"

The pastor said, "I'll do the best I can."

He prayed for grace, and he went into the backyard
where the little boy was. He put his arms around the lad
and said, "Billy, your mother is getting ready to take a
long trip."

And the little boy in his childish innocence looked into
the eyes of the pastor and said, "Pastor, there are two
questions I want to ask. One, how long will she be gone,

and two, when is she leaving?"

The pastor swallowed hard, and said, "Billy, your mother is not coming back." And then he looked up at a big tree overhead. It was in the latter part of September, and the leaves were beginning to change colors. He said, "When the leaves have all fallen from this big tree overhead, your mother will be gone."

Over the next two months he faithfully visited the lady. After nearly three months had ended he came to see her one day and she was very weak. She had lost weight and was hardly able to speak. He said to her, "How are you doing?"

She said with a faint smile, "Oh, I'm fine, but I don't see my little boy Billy very much. He stays in the backyard, and I am too weak to go to the window to see what he is doing. Would you go out and check on him?"

The pastor went into the backyard and could not find the little boy. He shouted, "Billy! Billy! Where are you?"

He then heard a quivering voice above as he turned and looked up into the tree, and there he saw the little boy with his pockets filled with leaves and several strands of string in his little hands. And then the little boy, choking back the tears, said, "Pastor, I'm up here trying to tie the leaves to the tree. I don't want the leaves to fall. I don't want Mama to leave."

APPLICATION

You cannot stop death no matter how hard you try, but because of Christ, you no longer have to fear death.

ADDITIONAL SCRIPTURES

Matthew 16:21-23; John 5:24; Romans 6:23;
1 Corinthians 15:55-57; 2 Timothy 1:9,10;
Revelation 21:1-4

Big Shot Lawyer

"This is love: not that we loved God, but that he loved us and sent his Son as an atoning sacrifice for our sins." 1 John 4:10

A new lawyer came to town. New town. New office. No clients. When he saw that someone was coming to his office, he immediately picked up his phone and said, "I'm flying to New York on the Timmons case. It looks like a biggie. And bring Paul in from New Jersey on the Pettus case. Also, I may be joining Houch, Staup and Patton as a partner. Gotta go now, someone just walked in." With that he hung up his phone, turned to the man, and said, "Now, how may I help you?"

The man replied: "I'm here to hook up the phone!"

 **APPLICATION**

You don't have to try to impress God! He loves you just the way you are! Because of His love and acceptance, you don't have to impress others to get your needs met.

ADDITIONAL SCRIPTURES

Deuteronomy 7:7,8; John 3:16; Romans 5:8-10; Ephesians 1:3-14; 2:4-10

You Tell Me

> **KEY VERSES**
>
> "'Are not five sparrows sold for two pennies? Yet not one of them is forgotten by God. Indeed, the very hairs of your head are numbered. Don't be afraid; you are worth more than many sparrows.'"
> Luke 12:6,7

Joe, a college student, was taking a course in ornithology, the study of birds. The night before the biggest test of the term, Joe spent all night studying. He had the textbook nearly memorized. He knew his class notes backward and forward. Joe was ready.

The morning of the test, Joe entered the auditorium and took a seat in the front row. On the table in the front was a row of ten stuffed birds. Each bird had a sack covering its body, and only the legs were showing. When class started, the professor announced that the students were to identify each bird by looking at its legs and give its common name, genus, species, habitat, mating habits, etc.

Joe looked at each of the birds' legs. They all looked the same to him. He started to get angry. He had stayed up all night studying for this test and now he had to identify birds by their legs. The more he thought about the situation, the angrier he got. Finally he reached his boiling point. He stood up, marched up to the professor's desk, crumpled up his exam paper and threw it on the desk. "What a ridiculous test!" he told the prof. "How could anyone tell the difference between these birds by looking at their legs? This exam is the biggest rip-off I've ever seen!"

With that, Joe turned and stormed toward the exit. The professor was a bit shocked, and it took him a moment to regain his composure. Then, just as Joe was about to walk out the door, the prof shouted out, "Wait a minute, young man, what's your name?"

Joe turned around, pulled up his pant legs and hollered, "You tell me, prof! You tell me!"

God knows each of us completely from the hairs on our heads to the freckles on our knees. But not only does he know us, he also loves us unconditionally.

Psalm 119:73; 139:1-16; Isaiah 44:24; Matthew 6:26; 10:29-31; Luke 12:12-31

She Knows Her Own

KEY VERSE

"O LORD, you have searched me and you know me."
Psalm 139:1

The guillemot is a small Arctic sea bird that lives on the rocky cliffs of the northern coastal regions. Guillemots flock together by the thousands in a very small area. In these extremely crowded conditions, the females lay their pear-shaped eggs side by side in a long row on a narrow ledge. But what is amazing is that although the eggs all look alike, the mother bird can identify the eggs she laid. She knows her own eggs so well that when even one of them is moved, she will find it and return it to its original location.

APPLICATION

God knows you even better than you know yourself. And guess what? He loves you anyway!

God's Love

ADDITIONAL SCRIPTURES

Psalms 139:1-16; Isaiah 49:15,16; Matthew 10:29,30;
John 3:16; 5:12,13; Romans 5:8; Ephesians 2:4,5; 3:17-19;
1 John 4:7-10

God's Love

Won't You Help Me?

KEY VERSE

"The Lord himself goes before you and will be with you; he will never leave you nor forsake you. Do not be afraid; do not be discouraged."
Deuteronomy 31:8

In 1989 an earthquake hit Armenia. Over 30,000 people were killed in a matter of minutes. After the quake, a father left the safety of his house and rushed to the school where he knew his son was at the time of the earthquake. When he arrived, he found that the building had been leveled.

He had once made a promise to his son: "No matter what, I'll always be there for you!" As he looked at the pile of debris, he felt hopeless and tears filled his eyes. What could he possibly do? But he kept remembering the commitment he had made to his son.

He remembered where his son's classroom was, in the back right corner of the building, and he rushed to the spot and started digging through the rubble. As he was digging, other heartbroken parents arrived. They were crying and saying, "My son!" "My daughter!" Others tried to pull him away from the debris, saying, "It's too late! They're dead! You can't help. Go home! Face reality, there's nothing you can do! You're just going to make things worse!"

But to each person he responded, "Won't you help me?" and continued to dig for his son, stone by stone.

The fire chief tried to pull him away, telling him fires were breaking out and explosions were happening all

around them. But the loving, caring Armenian father responded, "Won't you help me?"

The police told him he was endangering others and should go home, but again he replied, "Won't you help me?" No one helped.

Courageously he proceeded alone. He dug for eight hours…12 hours…24 hours…36 hours…then, in the 40th hour, he pulled back a boulder and heard his son's voice. He screamed his son's name, "ARMAND!"

He heard back, "Dad! It's me Dad! I told the other kids not to worry. I told them that if you were alive, you'd save me and when you saved me, they'd be saved. You promised, 'No matter what, I'll always be there for you!' You did it, Dad!"

There were 13 other children still alive with Armand. When the building collapsed, it had made a wedge like a triangle, and saved their lives.

Armand's father said to his son, "Come on out, boy!"

"No, Dad! Let the other kids out first, 'cause I know you'll get me! No matter what, I know you'll be there for me!"

APPLICATION

Have you ever given up on someone—believing that they were beyond hope? Remember God never gives up on you and you should never give up on anyone else.

ADDITIONAL SCRIPTURES

Deuteronomy 31:6; Luke 15:1-7; 18:3-27

I'll Hold You Close

KEY VERSE

"Even though I walk through the valley of the shadow of death, I will fear no evil, for you are with me; your rod and your staff, they comfort me."
Psalm 23:4

Solomon Rosenberg and his family were placed in one of the Nazi work camps where every person who could no longer work was taken to the gas ovens. The first in his family to be gassed were his aged parents—who were well into their 80s and very soon broke under the inhumane conditions of long hours, lack of decent food and miserable hygienic conditions.

Solomon knew that the next to go in his family would probably be their youngest son David, who was slightly crippled and was able to work less and less. Each morning the family was separated for their work assignments. At night the father would return with fear and trembling, wondering whether this might be the day that David would be taken. As he entered the barracks his eyes would quickly seek out his little boy David, his oldest boy Jacob and then the mother of his children.

At last the night came that he had feared. As he walked into the barracks, he could see none of his family and he became frantic. His eyes searched again for the precious faces of his family and then at last he saw the figure of his oldest boy Jacob, huddled over and weeping. But he still could not see little David or his wife. He hurried to Jacob and said, "Son, tell me it isn't so. Did they take David today?"

"Yes, Papa, they came to take David. They said he could no longer do his work.

"But Mama, where is Mama? She is still strong. Surely they wouldn't take Mama, too?"

And Jacob looked at his father through tearful eyes and said, "Papa, Papa. When they came to take David, he was afraid. And he cried. And so Mama said to David, 'Don't cry David. I will go with you and hold you close.' And so Mama went with David to the death chamber so he wouldn't be afraid."

You never have to face difficult times alone. God is always with you, holding you close.

Deuteronomy 31:6; Isaiah 41:13,14; Daniel 3:23-25; Matthew 28:20; Hebrews 13:5,6

I Knew You Would Come

KEY VERSE

"'Surely I am with you always, to the very end of the age.'" Matthew 28:20

There were two friends who served together during World War I. They spent much of the war involved in trench warfare, suffering from terrible living conditions and being constantly under fire. The closeness of the trenches and the terror of the war drew these two friends closer and closer together. They talked about life, their families, their hopes and about their future—when and if they returned home.

During one battle when the troops had left their trenches and charged the enemy, Jim was severely wounded and fell on the battlefield. Bill made it back to the trench. As the enemy's shelling continued, Jim lay suffering, all alone, in the no-man's land between the trenches.

As the shelling continued, Bill wanted to go to his friend so he could comfort him and encourage him as only a friend could do, but the officer in charge refused to let Bill leave the trench because it was too dangerous. But when the officer turned his back, Bill left the trench and began to make his way toward his friend. Shells exploded all around him, but he continued. Finally he made it to Jim.

He managed to drag Jim back to the trench, but it was too late. His friend died in his arms. The officer, seeing that he had died, looked at Bill and said, "Well, was it worth the risk?"

Without hesitation Bill said, "Yes, sir, it was. My friend's last words made it more than worth it. He looked up at me and said, 'I knew you would come.'"

Christ will never leave you alone and wounded on life's battlefield. He'll always be right beside you.

Deuteronomy 31:6; Psalm 23:4; Isaiah 41:13; Daniel 3; Matthew 1:23; Hebrews 13:5,6

God's Presence Through Difficulties

Pillsbury Doughboy Wanted for Attempted Murder

A lady named Linda went to Arkansas to visit her in-laws, and while there, went to a store. She parked next to a car with a woman sitting in it. The woman's eyes were closed and she had her hands behind her head and it looked like she was sleeping.

When Linda came out of the store a while later, she again saw the woman. Her hands were still behind her head, but her eyes were open. They looked very strange, so Linda tapped on the window and asked, "Are you okay?"

The woman answered, "I've been shot in the head, and I am holding my brains in."

Linda didn't know what to do, so she ran into the store, and had someone call the paramedics. When they arrived they had to break into the car because the door was locked. When they got in, they found that the woman had bread dough on the back of her head and in her hands.

A Pillsbury refrigerated biscuit can had apparently exploded from the heat in the car. It made a loud explosion like that of a gunshot and hit her in the head. When she reached back to find what it was, she felt the dough and thought it was her brains. She passed out from fright at first, then had attempted to hold her "brains" in.

God's Presence Through Difficulties

APPLICATION

Too often we worry about situations and imagine the worst possible outcome, when we should trust God.

ADDITIONAL SCRIPTURES

Proverbs 12:25; Matthew 6:25-27; John 14:27; 1 Peter 5:7

The Bumblebee

KEY VERSE

"I can do everything through him who gives me strength." Philippians 4:13

In briefing rooms of American air bases during World War II there were posters with the following inscription on them:

> By all known laws which can be proved on paper and in the wind tunnel—the bumblebee cannot fly. The size of his wings in relation to his body, according to aeronautical and mathematical science, simply means that he cannot fly. It is an impossibility. But of course, the bumblebee doesn't know about these rules so he goes ahead and flies anyway.

APPLICATION ——————

Rather than looking at all the obstacles and listening to everyone tell you what can't be done, realize that you can do whatever God calls you to do, relying on *His* strength rather than your own.

ADDITIONAL SCRIPTURES

1 Corinthians 1:27,28; 2 Corinthians 12:9,10;
Ephesians 3:16-19; James 2:5

God's Gifts to Us

God's Power and Strength

God's Gifts to Us

God's Power and Strength

A Different Perspective

In the year 1870, the Methodist churches in Indiana were having their annual conference. At one point, the president of the college where they were meeting addressed the group and told them they were living in a very exciting age. He said he believed that they were coming into a time of great inventions and that he believed, for example, that men would some day fly through the air like birds.

The presiding bishop didn't think much of this statement. As a matter of fact, he called it heresy and said that the Bible says that flight is reserved for angels so there would be no such talk there.

When the bishop got home, he told his family about what the president had said and how ridiculous it was. But his two young sons Wilbur and Orville looked at things from a different perspective than their father, Bishop Wright. And of course you know the rest of the story. But I wonder, would the Wright brothers have invented the airplane if they had not had a vision planted in their heads by way of one not-so-visionary father?

APPLICATION

It is impossible to fully imagine what God has in store for those who love Him.

ADDITIONAL SCRIPTURES

Isaiah 64:4; Jeremiah 29:11; Mark 9:23,24; 11:22-24; Ephesians 3:20

God's Gifts to Us

God's Power and Strength

Some Things Are Immovable

KEY VERSE

"Your word, O LORD, is eternal; it stands firm in the heavens." Psalm 119:89

Two battleships were on maneuvers in severe weather for several days. One evening as night fell on the foggy sea, the captain decided to stay on the bridge to keep an eye on things. The lookout on the wing of the bridge reported a light bearing on the starboard bow.

The captain asked if it were steady or moving astern. The lookout replied, "Steady, Captain." That meant they were on a collision course.

The captain called to the signalman, "Signal that ship to change its course 20 degrees to the north."

Back came this signal: "Change your course 20 degrees to the south."

The captain said, "Send: I am a captain. Change your course 20 degrees to the north."

The reply came back, "I am a Seaman, Second Class. Change your course 20 degrees south immediately."

By this time the captain was furious. He said, "Send: I am a battleship. Change your course 20 degrees north."

Back came the message, "Change your course 20 degrees south. I am a lighthouse."

APPLICATION

God's Word is the immovable standard by which all other things should be judged. If there is a difference between your truth and God's Truth, His Word always remains the same; your opinions must be the ones to change.

ADDITIONAL SCRIPTURES

Isaiah 40:8 (also 1 Peter 1:24); 55:10,11; Matthew 5:18; 24:35; Mark 13:31; Hebrews 13:8; 1 John 2:17

God's Gifts to Us

God's Grace

The Trial of Rudolf Hess

KEY VERSE

"For all have sinned and fall short of the glory of God." Romans 3:23

Perhaps the most famous trials in history were known as the Nuremberg Trials, the trials of the Nazi war criminals of World War II. One of the masterminds of probably the worst of all concentration camps—Auschwitz—was Rudolf Hess. His trial was broadcast all over the world. During the trial witness after witness came forward to the stand to relive the worst atrocities known to mankind. Witness after witness told of the brutality, the killings, the fear, the gas chambers, the crematorium, and of Hess in the middle of it all.

As the trial came to a close, the day of justice had come. On the day of the reading of the verdict, Rudolf Hess entered the room, awaiting his fate. The crowd and the media grew silent. The verdict came: GUILTY! As the verdict was read, weeping could be heard from different locations in the room. Some were silently crying, others openly weeping and wailing.

As the courtroom emptied, a reporter stopped one of the witnesses. He asked, "I can understand the emotion you must be feeling at this moment. Is it because justice has finally been served? Is it because now there is finally an end to the horror and the pain? Why is it that you are filled with such emotion?" The man stopped and looked long into the eyes of the reporter, and as he wiped his face he replied, "It has nothing to do with any of those. I weep because as I stood there looking into his eyes, I saw myself."

God's Grace

We are *all* sinners, deserving death. We are no better than the worst of all men. Given the right place, the right time, and the right circumstances, we could also be the worst of all sinners. Yet, while we were still sinners, Christ died for us. He took our place so that we might have new life.

APPLICATION

Everyone is capable of evil. God demonstrates the depth of His love in that through Christ's death on a cross even sinners are forgiven.

ADDITIONAL SCRIPTURES

Genesis 3:1-23; Psalm 143:2; Ecclesiastes 7:20; Isaiah 53:6,10; Hosea 6:7; John 3:16; Romans 3:22-24; 5:8

God's Gifts to Us

God's Grace

Recognized

"You are all sons of God through faith in Christ Jesus, for all of you who were baptized into Christ have clothed yourselves with Christ."
Galatians 3:26,27

As a shepherd was tending his sheep, two wolves attacked. One of the wolves killed the mother of one of the youngest lambs while the other wolf killed a small lamb as its mother looked on helplessly.

The shepherd finally succeeded in driving the wolves away, but he was left with a terrible problem. He had lost one mother and one small lamb, and he was in danger of losing a second lamb because its mother had been killed and none of the other sheep would nurse the lamb because it was not their own. Then the shepherd came up with a plan.

He took the skin of the dead lamb and put it over the live lamb. In doing this, he caused the mother, who had lost her little lamb, to recognize the lamb, who had lost its mother, as her own. So the mother accepted the little lamb, nursed it and it became her own.

God's Grace

APPLICATION

Christians are accepted in God's sight because they are clothed in the righteousness of Christ.

ADDITIONAL SCRIPTURES

Isaiah 61:10; Zechariah 3:1-4; Romans 13:14;
Ephesians 4:22-24; Hebrews 10:19; Revelation 19:7,8

How About a Nice Swim to Hawaii?

KEY VERSES

"For it is by grace you have been saved, through faith—and this not from yourselves, it is the gift of God—not by works, so that no one can boast."
Ephesians 2:8,9

Imagine that everyone in the United States is lined up on the shore of California and told that they have to either swim to Hawaii or die. There would be all kinds of people there of different shapes, sizes, nationalities, etc.

There would be the 500-pound man who can barely walk across the room without getting out of breath. As he begins to walk out into the water, a big wave knocks him over and he can't get up so he gargles salt water and drowns.

Then there would be the middle-aged guy who used to be a great swimmer. He begins to swim, but it isn't long before he begins to get tired. He practices the dead man's float he learned in Boy Scouts. He tries to keep going, but eventually he gives out. He too gargles salt water and drowns.

Then there would be the girl from the high school swim team. She has been swimming every day of her life for the past 10 years. She is in excellent physical condition. She begins to swim slowly and steadily—one mile, two miles, ten miles—but she begins to get cramps in her

tired muscles. She can't go on. She too gargles salt water and drowns.

Then there would be a marathon swimmer, like the guys who swim the English Channel. He would start out swimming strong and steady. He passes the 10-mile mark, the 20-mile mark and even the 50-mile mark, but eventually, he too begins to wear down. The waves take their toll and he finally gargles salt water and drowns.

Although some swimmers are much better than others, there is not a single swimmer, no matter how great, who can swim all the way to Hawaii.

Just as the best swimmer can't swim all the way to Hawaii from California, even the best person in the world can't get into heaven on the basis of his or her good works. It is only God's grace that makes the journey to heaven possible.

Psalm 143:1,2; Ecclesiastes 7:20; Romans 3:22-26; 4:2-8; Galatians 2:16; 2 Timothy 1:8-10; Titus 3:3-5

Broad Jumping the Grand Canyon

KEY VERSES

"But when the kindness and love of God our Savior appeared, he saved us, not because of righteous things we had done, but because of his mercy."
Titus 3:4,5

For the sake of illustration, imagine for a minute that every person in the United States is taken to the edge of the Grand Canyon and told they are going to be killed unless they can broad jump the canyon. One by one people begin to try, beginning with the least fit person and moving up to the most fit.

Some people would not have the strength to even jump an inch off the ground; when they'd try, they would roll down the side of the canyon. Others who are in better shape might jump four feet. A high school athlete might jump six feet. The broad-jumping champion of the world might jump 25 feet. But no one is going to jump the canyon. It doesn't matter what kind of physical shape they are in.

God's Grace

_____ APPLICATION

No one is ever going to be accepted by God and get into heaven on the basis of what they do. Some may do better than others, but no one is perfect.

_____ ADDITIONAL SCRIPTURES

Psalm 143:1,2; Ecclesiastes 7:20; Romans 3:22-28; 4:2-8; Galatians 2:8,9; Ephesians 2:4-9; 2 Timothy 1:8-10; Titus 3:4-7

The Touch of the Master's Hand

KEY VERSE

"Create in me a pure heart, O God, and renew a steadfast spirit within me." Psalm 51:10

It was battered and scarred, and the auctioneer
Thought it scarcely worth his while,
To waste much time on the old violin,
But held it up with a smile.

"What am I bid for this old violin?
Who will start the bidding for me?
A dollar, a dollar, who'll make it two?
Two dollars, and who'll make it three?

"Three dollars, once; three dollars twice,
Going for three," But no;
From the back of the room a gray-haired man
Came forward and picked up the bow.

Then wiping the dust from the old violin,
And tightening up all the strings,
He played a melody pure and sweet,
As sweet as the angels sing.

The music ceased, and the auctioneer
With a voice that was quiet and low
Said, "What am I bid for the old violin?"
And he held it up with the bow.

"A thousand dollars, and who'll make it two?
Two thousand! And who'll make it three?
Three thousand, once; three thousand, twice;
And going and gone," said he.

The people cheered, but some of them said,
"We do not quite understand,
What changes its worth?" Came the reply,
"The touch of a master's hand."

And many a man with life out of tune,
And battered and scarred with sin,
Is auctioned cheap to a thoughtless crowd,
Much like the old violin.

A "mess of pottage," a glass of wine;
A game, and he shuffles along.
He's going once, and he's going twice,
He's going and almost gone.

But the Master comes, and the thoughtless crowd
Never quite understands
The worth of a soul, and the change that's wrought
By the touch of the Master's hand.

                                    —Myra Brooks Welch

APPLICATION

Only God can take a life that is battered and scarred by
sin and by His grace turn it into one that is beautiful and
whole again.

ADDITIONAL SCRIPTURES

Psalm 51:7-13; Isaiah 1:18; 2 Corinthians 5:17

I Am Grimaldi

KEY VERSE

"'I have come that they may have life, and that they may have it more abundantly.'" John 10:10, *NKJV*

In the early 1800s in Manchester, England, an unhappy and depressed middle-aged man, while traveling, visited a physician who had been recommended to him.

"What's the nature of your ailment?" the physician asked.

The sad-faced man told the physician he was suffering from a hopeless illness. He was in terror of the world around him and nothing gave him pleasure or amused him or gave him a reason to live. "If you can't help me," he told the physician, "I'm afraid I will kill myself."

The physician tried to reassure the man. He told the man that he could be cured. He encouraged him to get out of himself, to find things that would amuse him, cheer him up and make him laugh.

The patient said, "Where can I go to find such a diversion?"

The physician replied, "The circus is in town tonight. Go see Grimaldi the clown. Grimaldi is the funniest man alive. He will cure you."

The sad-faced patient looked up and said, "Doctor, I am Grimaldi. I am Grimaldi."

God's Gifts to Us

Abundant Life

_____  **APPLICATION**

True purpose, meaning and joy only comes from knowing Jesus Christ.

_____  **ADDITIONAL SCRIPTURES**

Nehemiah 8:10-12; Proverbs 15:13,15,30; 17:22; John 15:9-11; 2 Corinthians 5:17; Philippians 4:4-7

Here Comes the Cat!

KEY VERSE

"For I know the plans I have for you," declares the LORD, "plans to prosper you and not to harm you, plans to give you hope and a future."
Jeremiah 29:11

This is a story of a "Mouse Universe." In this universe lived many, many mice. They were the only occupants of Mouse Universe, although they knew that somewhere, someplace was a giant cat. They went about their every-day lives day in and day out with the sneaky suspicion that any day the giant cat would come and devour them.

Sure enough, one day the big cat came. The word spread like wildfire and the mice from all the corners of the universe scrambled to save their lives. They ran under rocks, hid behind trees and buried themselves under leaves. No mouse was safe. Every mouse trembled.

When the giant cat appeared, he had with him a huge red wagon filled with all kinds of delicious cheese. The cat came to give the cheese to all the mice! They finally came out and they had a great party. The cat was a good cat and only wanted to be friends with the mice.

God's Gifts to Us

Abundant Life

APPLICATION

Many people see God as a giant killjoy in the sky trying to keep people from having fun, so they avoid Him. But Jesus came that we might enjoy life to the fullest extent.

ADDITIONAL SCRIPTURES

Genesis 3:8; John 10:10; Romans 5:17; Jude 24,25

How to Catch a Monkey

KEY VERSE

"'For whoever wants to save his live will lose it, but whoever loses his life for me and for the gospel will save it.'" Mark 8:35

They say one way people catch monkeys in the jungles of Africa is by getting a large, strong gourd and cutting a hole in the side of it just barely big enough for a monkey's hand to fit in. Then they firmly attach the gourd to the limb of a tree so it can't be moved. They then place some of the monkey's favorite nuts inside the gourd.

When the monkey discovers the gourd he will slip his hand in and grab a handful of nuts. Then he'll try to pull his hand out, but he won't be able to. He'll keep trying and trying and trying, but he'll never let go of the nuts. Finally when he is completely tired out, someone walks up, throws a net over him and carries him off.

Abundant Life

_____  APPLICATION

We try to hold on to our way of life so tightly that we miss out on the opportunity for the abundant life that Christ offers.

_____  ADDITIONAL SCRIPTURES

Matthew 19:16-22; John 12:25

God's Gifts to Us

Abundant Life

Yates Pool

"'I have come that they may have life, and have it to the full.'" John 10:10

In West Texas is a famous oil field known as the Yates Pool. During the Depression, this field was a sheep ranch owned by a man named Yates. Mr. Yates was not able to make enough money on his ranching operation to pay the principal and interest on the mortgage, so he was in danger of losing his ranch. With little money for clothes or food, his family like many others had to live on a government subsidy.

Day after day, as he grazed his sheep, he wondered how he would be able to pay his bills. Then a seismographic crew from an oil company came into the area and told Mr. Yates that there might be oil on his land. They asked permission to drill a wildcat well, and he signed a lease contract.

At 1,115 feet they struck a huge oil reserve. The first well came in at 80,000 barrels a day. Many of the later wells were more than twice as large. Thirty years after the first well was drilled, all the wells still had the potential of pumping 125,000 barrels of oil a day. And Mr. Yates owned it all! The day he purchased the land he received the oil and mineral rights, yet he was living on relief. A multimillionaire living in poverty! The problem? He did not know the oil was there. He owned it, but he did not know it.

Abundant Life

APPLICATION

Christ came that you might have a full and meaningful life, yet many are not experiencing that joy even though it is right at their fingertips.

ADDITIONAL SCRIPTURES

Luke 15:11-32; John 1:4; 3:14-16; Romans 8:32; Ephesians 3:8; 4:22-24; Colossians 1:27; 2:9,10; 1 John 3:1,2

A Strange Bird

KEY VERSE

"For we are God's workmanship, created in Christ Jesus to do good works, which God prepared in advance for us to do." Ephesians 2:10

There in the middle of the chickens was an eagle. It was a full-grown, king-of-all-birds eagle! But he was scratching in the dirt looking for worms, insects and seeds. He was clucking and cackling and flapping his wings as he flew just a few feet at a time.

This eagle had a six-foot wing span that would allow him to fly among the clouds, but instead he was just fluttering around on the ground. His keen eyesight and sharp talons were supposed to make him a threat to every small bird and mammal anywhere near him. Yet the only thing he was a threat to was some unsuspecting worm he might happen to unearth.

Why in the world was this eagle acting like a chicken? Here is the story: An Indian brave found the eagle egg and he didn't know what to do with it, so he put it in the nest of a prairie chicken. The eaglet hatched and grew up with the other chicks. He never saw another eagle—only chickens. All his life he thought he was a prairie chicken. He mimicked their every move.

One day when the eagle was growing old, he looked up into the sky and saw an eagle soaring on the wind far above him. "What a beautiful bird!" the eagle said to the chicken next to him. "What is it?"

"That's an eagle—the king of all birds," the chicken clucked, "but don't give it a second thought. You could never be like him."

So the eagle never gave it a second thought, and died thinking he was a prairie chicken.

Rather than comparing yourself to those around you, seek to understand God's plan for your life.

Psalm 139:1-15; Jeremiah 29:11; 1 Corinthians 2:9,10; 2 Corinthians 10:12

The "Sheep-Lion"

KEY VERSE

"Therefore, if anyone is in Christ, he is a new creation; the old has gone, the new has come!"
2 Corinthians 5:17

You'll beam with PRIDE

Once upon a time there was a lion who had been lost just after his birth. Fortunately for him he was rescued and subsequently raised by a mother sheep.

She raised him just the way she raised her other sheep children. She taught him to eat grass. And although his teeth grew large and his jaw muscles bulged, he continued to eat grass.

She also taught him to baa-baa like a sheep. Although his lungs grew big and strong, he still would baa-baa. And of course, she taught him to walk. And although he tiptoed around like a dainty sheep, he still seemed to have an urge to do so much more.

One day, after he had grown into a strong, mature lion, he happened upon a group of lions. He noticed how they roared loudly and convincingly and how they galloped, leaped and ran the way their powerful legs were meant to do. They shared a piece of meat with him and it tasted uniquely sweet to his massive teeth and jaws. And then it hit him. "I'm a lion!" he said. And with that, he ran to join the other lions.

APPLICATION

Until you come to know Christ, you will always feel mis-placed. It is Jesus who gives you meaning and purpose in life.

ADDITIONAL
SCRIPTURES

Genesis 1:27; Psalm 139:1-4,13-16; Isaiah 43:7;
Luke 19:10

Our
Relationship
with
God

Making Choices

The Alcoholic Dad

KEY VERSE

"""So then each of us will give an account of himself to God.""" Romans 14:12

There once was a man who was a desperate alcoholic. He had been married and divorced twice, was in and out of jail and could never hold down a decent job. His life was pathetic.

From his first marriage, though, he had twin sons. One grew up to be a prominent and well-respected lawyer who was happily married and the father of three children.

He was a leader in his church and considered a "pillar of the community."

His brother, on the other hand, was just the opposite. He, like his father, was divorced twice, in and out of jail and could not land a good, long-lasting job. In addition, he suffered from a 15-year alcohol addiction.

One day a reporter asked them, "Why are you the way you are?"

They both gave the same answer: "I am the way I am because of my father."

The first man was an overcomer. He decided that he was not going to let the mistakes of his father ruin his life.

The second son gave in and said to himself, "What chance do I have?" He was defeated before he even started.

APPLICATION

You can give excuses and blame others for not being what you ought to be, or you can work to become all God intends you to be and give the credit to Him.

ADDITIONAL SCRIPTURES

John 15:1-8; Romans 11:17-21; 2 Corinthians 5:17; Ephesians 4:22-24; 1 Timothy 1:15,16

The Zode

KEY VERSES

"'No one can serve two masters. Either he will hate the one and love the other, or he will be devoted to the one and despise the other.'" Matthew 6:24

Did I ever tell you about the young Zode,
Who came to two signs at the fork in the road?
One said to Place One, and the other, Place Two.
So the Zode had to make up his mind what to do.
Well...the Zode scratched his head, and his chin and
    his pants.
And he said to himself, "I'll be taking a chance
If I go to Place One. Now, that place may be hot!
And so, how do I know if I'll like it or not?
On the other hand though, I'll be sort of a fool
If I go to Place Two and find it too cool.
In that case I may catch a chill and turn blue!
So, maybe Place One is the best, not Place Two,
But then again, what if Place One is too high?
I may catch a terrible earache and die!
So Place Two may be best! On the other hand though...
What might happen to me if Place Two is too low?
I might get some very strange pain in my toe!
So Place One may be best," and he started to go.
Then he stopped, and he said, "On the other hand
    though...
On the other hand...other hand...other hand though..."
And for 36 hours and a half that poor Zode
Made starts and made stops at the fork in the road.
Saying, "Don't take a chance. No! You may not be right."
Then he got an idea that was wonderfully bright!

"Play safe!" cried the Zode. "I'll play safe. I'm no dunce!
I'll simply start out for both places at once!"
And that's how the Zode who would not take a chance
Got no place at all with a split in his pants.[1]

You can't go in two directions at one time; you can't live
for yourself and for God at the same time.

Joshua 24:15; Luke 16:13; Ephesians 4:14; James 1:6-8

Note:
1. Theodor Geisel (Dr. Seuss), "The Zode" (unpublished manuscript).

Crowd Followers

"'Enter through the narrow gate. For wide is the gate and broad is the road that leads to destruction, and many enter through it. But small is the gate and narrow the road that leads to life, and only a few find it.'" Matthew 7:13,14

Look at those Crowd Followers, now aren't they a bunch?
Following the crowd from breakfast to lunch.
Never asking, "Where are we going?"
Just riding the current wherever it's flowing.

They say to themselves, "Now this sure is a breeze,
Following the crowd is as easy as you please."
They never stop to consider where all this will end;
They just keep on following all of their friends.

"Everyone else must know where we're heading,
So why should I do any fretting?
I'll just follow the crowd all day and all night.
I'm sure everything will turn out all right.

"Everyone is laughing and having such fun,
Why, not following the crowd would really be dumb.
I really don't care where all this may end;
I just want to keep having fun with my friends."

But every road must come to an end.
The Crowd Followers too have to round the last bend.
And when they do they will come face to face
With the Creator and Designer of the whole human race.

And He'll not ask what the crowd has to say,
For each person will have to speak for themselves that day.

And when everything has been said and been done,
The crowd again will march forward as one.

No one will, that day, want to follow their friends,
Because they know destruction will be their end.
But because they spent their life following the crowd,
On that final day no turning back will be allowed.

Author Unknown

If you decide to follow the crowd in life, you need to ask yourself one question: "Do I really want to go where the crowd is heading?"

Exodus 23:2; Joshua 24:15; Daniel 1:5,8-17; Luke 13:24-30; John 21:19

Jesus Is in My Heart

KEY VERSE

"'Blessed are the pure in heart, for they will see God.'" Matthew 5:8

CHECK-UP TIME!

A little four-year-old girl was at the pediatrician's office for a check-up. As the doctor looked into her ears with an otoscope, he asked, "Do you think I'll find Big Bird in here?" The little girl didn't say a word.

Next, the doctor took a tongue depressor and looked down her throat. He asked, "Do you think I'll find the Cookie Monster down there?" Again the little girl did not respond.

Then the doctor put a stethoscope to her chest. As he listened to her heartbeat, he asked, "Do you think I'll hear Barney in here?"

"Oh, no!" the little girl replied. "Jesus is in my heart. Barney's on my underpants."

APPLICATION

Everyone has the opportunity to have Jesus in their hearts. All you have to do is ask Him in.

ADDITIONAL SCRIPTURES

Psalm 24:3-5; Matthew 22:37,38; Luke 12:35,36;
John 14:12; Romans 8:9-11; Galatians 2:20;
Ephesians 3:16-19; Revelation 3:20

The Pardon: A Louisiana Court Case

KEY VERSE

"For the wages of sin is death, but the gift of God is eternal life in Christ Jesus our Lord."
Romans 6:23

In Louisiana, there was a trial that held the attention of the entire state. The year was 1982 and a man was condemned to die for the murder of a family. As he sat on death row, his attorneys frantically tried to secure a pardon for their client.

They used just about every means within their grasp. As the hour approached, all hope seemed to fade. Then unexpectedly, at 11:30 P.M., one-half hour before he was to die in the gas chamber, the governor of Louisiana extended a full pardon to the man.

The attorneys were overjoyed as they brought the news to their client. As they told him of his freedom something happened that brought the state of Louisiana to a standstill. He refused the pardon. At precisely 12:00 midnight, they strapped the man to the chair and within a few moments he was dead. The entire state was in shock. The man had a full pardon, yet chose to die anyway.

A fierce legal battle soon erupted over this issue: Was the man pardoned because the governor offered the pardon, or was he pardoned only when he accepted the pardon? The highest court in the state of Louisiana was the arena for the debate. Ultimately it was decided that the pardon cannot go into effect until it is accepted.

So it is with us. God offers us eternal life, a pardon from sin, yet too often we reject the pardon. God offers the pardon, but we need to accept it.

Our Relationship with God

Making Choices

APPLICATION

God laid the punishment for your sin on Jesus. All you have to do is acknowledge and accept God's gift—His pardon for your sins. What will you do with His gift of salvation?

ADDITIONAL SCRIPTURES

Joshua 24:15; John 3:16; Romans 8:10;
2 Corinthians 6:1,2; Galatians 2:20; 1 John 3:23;
Revelation 3:20

Christ Knocking

KEY VERSE

"'Here I am! I stand at the door and knock. If anyone hears my voice and opens the door, I will come in and eat with him, and he with me.'"
Revelation 3:20

In Saint Paul's Cathedral in London hangs Holman Hunt's artistic masterpiece, "The Light of the World." It is the picture of a cottage that is run down, and bushes and briars have grown up around it. The walkway is covered by weeds and grass, and the hinges are rusty and stained by the elements of nature.

Standing at the door, Jesus is holding a lantern in one hand which gives off light to every part of the picture, and He is knocking with the other hand. Most people refer to that picture as "Christ Waiting at the Door," or "Christ Knocking at the Door," but the artist himself named it "The Light of the World."

After Hunt completed that picture, a discerning critic said to him, "Mr. Hunt, you made a mistake. There is no handle on the door!"

The artist gently replied, "No, my friend, I did not make a mistake for there *is* a handle. The handle is on the inside."

Once a little girl and her father were standing at the cathedral looking at that beautiful picture. They were mesmerized as they gazed upon the picture, and they sought to understand and interpret its meaning. The two stood there in silence for five, ten and then fifteen minutes. The quietness was broken when the little girl in her childlike way asked a very simple question, "Daddy, did they ever let him in?"

APPLICATION

Christ stands knocking at the door of your heart. All you have to do is open the door and let Him in.

ADDITIONAL SCRIPTURES

Luke 12:35-40; John 14:20,23; 15:4; Romans 8:9-11; Galatians 2:20; Ephesians 3:16-19; 1 John 4:15,16

Time Will Tell

KEY VERSE

"What good is it for a man to gain the whole world, yet forfeit his soul?" Mark 8:36

In 1923 a meeting was held at the Edgewater Beach hotel in Chicago. Attending the meeting were nine of the world's most successful financiers: Charles Schwab, steel magnate; Samuel Insull, president of the largest utility company; Howard Hopson, president of the largest gas company; Arthur Cotton, the greatest wheat speculator; Richard Whitney, president of the New York Stock Exchange; Albert Fall, a member of the president's cabinet; Leon Fraser, president of the Bank of International Settlements; Jesse Livermore, the great "bear" on Wall Street; and Ivar Krueger, head of the most powerful monopoly.

Twenty-five years later, Charles Schwab had died in bankruptcy, and had lived his last five years on borrowed money; Samuel Insull had died a fugitive from justice and penniless in a foreign land; Howard Hopson was insane; Arthur Cotton had died abroad, insolvent; Richard Whitney had spent time in Sing Sing; Albert Fall had been pardoned so that he could die at home; Jesse Livermore, Ivar Krueger and Leon Fraser had all died by suicide.

Making Choices

It is possible to spend all your life trying to gain the world, only to lose your own soul in the process.

Matthew 6:24,28-33; Mark 8:34-38; Luke 12:15-21; 14:25-35; John 12:23-25; 1 Corinthians 1:18-31

The Same Old Otis

KEY VERSE

"Therefore, if anyone is in Christ, he is a new creation; the old has gone, the new has come!"
2 Corinthians 5:17

In one of the old Andy Griffith TV shows, Otis, the town drunk, got a letter telling him that he was to receive a large amount of money. There was one catch. He had to go for an interview and prove that he was worthy to receive the money.

Well Andy and Barney helped get Otis ready for his interview. They sobered him up, shaved him, got him a hair cut and bought him a new suit. He looked like a completely new person. He went for the interview and was given the money. But a few days later he came stumbling back into the jail, drunk. He had not shaved, his new suit was a mess. What happened? Nothing! That's right—nothing! Nothing had happened inside Otis. He was still the same drunk he was before. He had only been temporarily cleaned up on the outside.

APPLICATION

Unless Christ transforms you from the inside out, any changes you make to improve yourself only lead you back to where you started.

ADDITIONAL SCRIPTURES

John 1:12,13; Romans 6:4

Our Relationship with God

Obedience

A Conference in Hell

KEY VERSE

"Anyone...who knows the good he ought to do and doesn't do it, sins." James 4:17

NO HURRY!

It is said that a long time ago there was a conference in hell, and ol' Lucifer was plotting and scheming how he might catch the human race and keep them from God.

One fiendish lieutenant came to the master of evil and said, "If you will send me to earth I will tell the people that there is no heaven to be gained."

Lucifer said to him, "No, no! They'll never believe it because there is a little bit of heaven in every heart."

Another fiend came forward, darker and fowler than the first, and he said to Lucifer, "If you would send me to earth, I would convince the people that they can sin with immunity. That God would continue to love and forgive. That He would never, ever, ever judge anyone—even if they didn't repent. I will convince them of that."

The father of darkness said, "No! These humans must not be underestimated. They have a conscience and deep within the heart of every human is this sense of righteousness. Beneath all their protestations they know that evil will be punished. They know that good will triumph over evil."

A third lieutenant, from the very darkest pit, emerged into the shadow of Lucifer's countenance and said, "Master, if you would send me, I would tell them this: 'There is no hurry!'"

And Lucifer said, "Go."

APPLICATION

It is so easy to think that there is no hurry when it comes to making a decision about our relationship with God, yet none of us knows when our life might end.

ADDITIONAL SCRIPTURES

Joshua 24:15; Psalm 39:5; 144:3,4; Isaiah 2:22; James 4:13-17

Obedience

God Goes Before Us

KEY VERSE

"The one who calls you is faithful and he will do it."
1 Thessalonians 5:24

Pretend you are living in the following situation:

You are in a country where Christians are a distinct minority. The official policy is anti-Christian; in fact, a systematic program of harassment, imprisonment, torture, and in some cases, even execution is being carried out against believers. To complicate the situation, your country has recently lost a war and is living under an occupying force of foreign troops. This foreign power is theoretically neutral about religion, but is actually worried that the Christian minority may destabilize the situation. Economically, you, like most other Christians, are definitely lower-class, with no political or economic clout.

Now, as if just surviving weren't enough, the leader of the little team of Christians announces that you are going on a visitation evangelism program. He hands you three names to choose from. You read the names and almost fall over.

Number one is the secretary of the treasury of a powerful neighboring country. He has been visiting your capital for an economic conference. Number two is a leading official of the majority religion in your country, the man who is chiefly responsible for the campaign against Christians. Number three is one of the top officers of the occupying forces, a man known as a fair but tough administrator of the law.

Which would you choose? But now look at the book of Acts for a moment. We have almost the exact situation described above. In Acts 8, the Lord ordered a Christian, Philip, to go down into the Gaza Strip and meet an important government official from Ethiopia who was sitting in his chariot and reading. I'm sure Philip must have been reluctant. But when he got there, he found that this man was actually reading the book of Isaiah from the Old Testament and was trying to figure out whom the prophet was talking about. When Philip identified the subject of the passage as Jesus Christ, the man believed and was baptized on the spot!

In Acts 9, a man named Ananias had an even scarier assignment. The Lord said, "Go to the house of Judas on Straight Street and ask for a man from Tarsus named Saul" (v. 11). Ananias knew Saul's main priority was harassing Christians, but he went. When he got there, he found that Jesus Christ had already met Saul on the road to Damascus. Saul was waiting for someone to come and fill in the details about Jesus and tell him what to do next.

In Acts 10, the Lord told Peter to go to a Gentile army officer named Cornelius. Peter was so skeptical that God had to send a vision to convince him. Imagine the cultural gap. For a humble Jewish fisherman to go to the home of a leading Gentile army officer must have been a frightening affair. But again, when he got there, he found that Cornelius and all of his house had assembled and were waiting to hear Peter's message.[2]

Obedience

APPLICATION

When God instructs you to be a messenger, do not hesitate to be obedient, for He has prepared the way and will help you accomplish His will.

ADDITIONAL SCRIPTURES

John 6:44; Acts 8:26-40; 9:10-19; 10:1-8; Philippians 2:12,13; 1 Thessalonians 5:24

Note:
2. Leighton Ford, *Good News Is for Sharing* (Elgin, Ill.: David C. Cook, 1977), pp. 19-20.

Constitutional King or Prime Minister?

KEY VERSE

"'Not everyone who says to me, "Lord, Lord," will enter the kingdom of heaven, but only he who does the will of my Father who is in heaven.'"
Matthew 7:21

Star Treatment

The country of England has a constitutional queen and a prime minister. The queen has no power to make decisions. She is simply a figurehead. The prime minister, on the other hand, is the one who makes all the political decisions and holds all the power.

APPLICATION

Jesus Christ can be just the constitutional king of your life, or He can be the prime minister of your life, having the power to lead you where He would have you go. The choice is yours!

Our Relationship with God

Obedience

_____ ADDITIONAL SCRIPTURES

Matthew 24:45,46; Romans 6:14-18; 1 Corinthians 2:14—
3:3; 2 Corinthians 4:5; Ephesians 5:15-17;
Philippians 2:9-11; Colossians 1:10,16-18;
1 Timothy 6:11-16; James 1:22-25

Keeping up Appearances

KEY VERSE

"Am I now trying to win the approval of men, or of God? Or am I trying to please men? If I were still trying to please men, I would not be a servant of Christ." Galatians 1:10

The short story "The Necklace" by Guy de Maupassant tells of a young woman named Mathilde who desperately wants to be accepted by high society. Her husband is a common worker, but they are invited to an elegant ball. Mathilde, feeling that she has to make an impression on the people at the ball, borrows a beautiful necklace from a wealthy friend to wear. She is well accepted by the aristocracy at the ball and the evening would have been a total success if it were not for one small problem. She lost the borrowed necklace.

To keep from having to tell her wealthy friend and risk embarrassment, she talked her husband into replacing the lost necklace. He had to borrow nearly 40,000 francs, from every possible source he knew, in order to pay for the replacement necklace. Mathilde gave the replacement to her wealthy friend without telling her what had happened.

For the next ten years Mathilde and her husband both worked two jobs to pay back the money they had borrowed to replace the necklace. They wound up having to live in a slum because their home had to be sold to meet their obligations, but finally they were able to pay off the last of their debt.

One day Mathilde ran into the friend who had loaned her the necklace and the friend hardly recognized her because Mathilde looked so haggard from all the hard

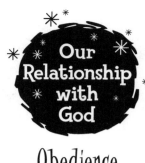

work. She confessed to her friend that she had lost her original necklace and had to work so hard to pay for the replacement. It was only then that she learned that the original necklace had been made, not with diamonds, but with fake gemstones! It was worth less than 500 francs. She and her husband had worked and suffered all those years simply because Mathilde had tried to keep up appearances.

APPLICATION

When you try to please people and keep up appearances rather than trying to please God, you will suffer needlessly.

ADDITIONAL SCRIPTURES

Matthew 6:5,16-18; 23:2-5; Romans 12:1,2;
Philippians 3:7-9; Colossians 2:16—3:4;
1 Timothy 4:12; 1 Peter 3:3,4; 1 John 2:15-17; 3:21-24

Seven Days of Hooray and Whoop-Dee-Doo

KEY VERSE

"The fear of the LORD is the beginning of knowledge, but fools despise wisdom and discipline." Proverbs 1:7

In Dr. James Dobson's book, *Emotions: Can You Trust Them?*, he tells a true story that happened at the high school his mother attended in the 1930s. The school was located in a small Oklahoma town, and their football team lost all the time, especially to archrivals. The students, the players and the people in the town were all depressed and dispirited from continually being defeated.

Finally a rich oil producer decided to take matters into his own hands after the team was defeated one Friday night. He offered to buy a brand new Ford for every football player and the coach if they won the game against their bitter rivals the coming week. The team went crazy. They cheered and shouted and for the next seven days they ate, drank and breathed football. The entire school caught football fever.

Finally, the big night arrived. Excitement was at an unprecedented high. They assembled on the sidelines, put their hands together and shouted a simultaneous "Rah!" Then they ran onto the field and were demolished, 38 to zero.

Our Relationship with God

Obedience

_____ APPLICATION

Success on the playing field takes hard work and discipline, just as in the Christian life.

_____ ADDITIONAL SCRIPTURES

Proverbs 5:23; 10:17; 12:1; 13:18; 23:23;
1 Corinthians 9:24-27; 2 Timothy 1:7; 2:5-7; 3:16,17;
Hebrews 12:7-11

Our Relationship with God

Obedience

You Can't Just Sit There

KEY VERSE

"If any of you lacks wisdom, he should ask God, who gives generously to all without finding fault, and it will be given to him." James 1:5

Larry Walters lives in a little suburb outside of Los Angeles just south of the Los Angeles Airport. Larry, who is a truck driver, used to spend his weekends in his backyard sitting in his favorite lawn chair with a six-pack and some peanut butter sandwiches.

Several years ago, when Larry was 33 years old, he was sitting around looking at all the fences around him in the subdivision where he lived when he got an idea. He decided he would go buy some weather balloons, fill them with helium and tie them to his lawn chair. He figured they would allow him to float 100 or so feet up in the air so that he could visit with all his neighbors, who lived behind all those fences, while he floated along. I'm not sure just how many six-packs he had consumed when the idea came to him, but he decided to take a BB gun with him so he could shoot out the balloons if he started to go too high and thus be able to maintain his altitude at about 100 feet above the subdivision.

He got 30 to 40 weather balloons and filled them with helium. He brought them to his house and tied them to his lawn chair. He went in the house and got another six-pack and a couple of peanut butter-and-jelly sandwiches and his BB gun. He took his supplies outside with him and sat down in his lawn chair which his friends were holding down for him. Then he said, "Let 'er go!" But he didn't go to only 100 feet. He went to 11,000 feet! He shot straight up in the air! As a matter of fact, he couldn't shoot out the balloons, because he was afraid he

would cause the chair to get off balance and he would fall out. And it just happened that he floated straight up into the landing pattern of Los Angeles Airport.

A Continental pilot of a DC-10 reported seeing a lawn chair floating by. You can only imagine the control tower wanting to know how many six-packs the pilot had consumed. Can you imagine the pilot coming on the intercom and saying, "If you will look out the right side of the plane, you will see a man in his lawn chair, eating peanut butter sandwiches and drinking a beer."

Larry Walters was holding on for dear life. Eventually they sent helicopters up. They stopped all takeoffs and landings at the airport while they got this 33-year-old truck driver and his lawn chair down from 11,000 feet. When he was finally back on the ground, he was surrounded by a huge crowd. The police were there, the helicopter crew, the television crews and all the other reporters.

One reporter stuck a microphone in his face and said, "I have three questions to ask you. Were you scared?"

"What kind of question is that? Wouldn't *you* be scared if you were floating around in a lawn chair at 11,000 feet?"

Then the reporter asked, "Are you going to do it again?"

To which he got a strong "No!"

Finally he asked him, "What in the world made you do it the first time?"

To that Larry Walters said, "Well, you can't just sit there."

When you allow your own thinking rather than God's wisdom to guide you, you will inevitably end up off course.

Proverbs 1:7; 2:1-11; 13:16, 26:12; Daniel 2:19-23; 1 Corinthians 14:20; Ephesians 1:17; 4:14; James 1:5-7

Strength for the Future

"Anyone who lives on milk, being still an infant, is not acquainted with the teaching about righteousness. But solid food is for the mature, who by constant use have trained themselves to distinguish good from evil." Hebrews 5:13,14

Each fall, during breeding season, the male Alaskan bull moose battle for dominance. They fight with all their might against one another, and their antlers, their only weapon, take a pounding. If one of the antlers is broken, defeat is almost ensured.

Almost always the heftiest moose with the largest and strongest antlers wins. For that reason, the outcome of the battle is usually determined during the preceding summer which might be called "training camp." It is during the summer when the moose eat nonstop. The ones who consume the best diet for strengthening their antlers and building muscle will end up defeating those who ate an inadequate diet when the fall battles begin. An inadequate diet that leaves the moose with weak antlers and small muscles most assuredly means defeat.

APPLICATION

For spiritual strength you must have an adequate diet of God's Word, prayer and Christian fellowship.

ADDITIONAL SCRIPTURES

1 Corinthians 3:1-3; Ephesians 4:14-16; Hebrews 5:11-14; 1 Peter 2:1-3

We've Always Done It

KEY VERSE

"Therefore do not be foolish, but understand what the Lord's will is." Ephesians 5:17

A man walked by and saw a sentry standing guard for no apparent reason, so he approached the sentry and asked him why he was standing in that particular place.

The sentry replied, "I don't know. I'm just following orders."

So the man went to the captain of the guard and asked him why the sentry was posted in that place.

"I don't know," replied the captain, "we're just following orders."

This aroused the captain's curiosity, so he went and asked those in authority over him. They too had no idea why the guard was posted there so they asked the king. The king didn't know either so he summoned his wise men and asked them.

After a little research they came back to the king with an answer. About one hundred years earlier, Catherine the Great had planted a rosebush and had ordered a sentry placed there to protect it. The rosebush had been dead for over eighty years, but the sentry still stood guard.

APPLICATION

Never do anything just because it has always been done that way. Instead, you should consider what God would have you do in each situation.

ADDITIONAL SCRIPTURES

Exodus 17:1-6; Numbers 20:1-12; Psalm 127:1; Romans 12:1,2; Ephesians 5:15-17

The Chicken and the Pig

KEY VERSE

"'If anyone would come after me, he must deny himself and take up his cross and follow me.'"
Mark 8:34

One day Farmer John's pig was talking to his chicken. "What can we do for Farmer John to show our appreciation for all he has done for us?" the pig asked.

"I don't know," replied the chicken. "What do you think?"

They thought for a moment and then the chicken spoke up: "We could serve him a huge thank-you breakfast with scrambled eggs and bacon!"

The pig thought for a moment and then said, "Oh sure, that's easy for you to say. For you it's a small sacrifice, but for me it's total commitment."

Commitment

APPLICATION

The Christian life does not call for a small sacrifice; it demands a total commitment.

ADDITIONAL SCRIPTURES

Matthew 10:37-39; 16:24-26; (also Mark 8:34-38; Luke 14:25-33); Romans 12:1,2; Philippians 1:21

Letter from a Communist

KEY VERSE

"We are therefore Christ's ambassadors, as though God were making his appeal through us. We implore you on Christ's behalf: Be reconciled to God." 2 Corinthians 5:20

A university student, while visiting Mexico, discovered in the Communist workers there a true dedication to their cause. Shortly afterwards he wrote the following letter to his fiancée, breaking off their engagement.

> We Communists have a high casualty rate. We're the ones who get shot at and hung and lynched and tarred and feathered and jailed and slandered and ridiculed and fired from our jobs. We are in every way made as uncomfortable as possible. A certain percentage of us get killed or imprisoned. We live in virtual poverty. We turn back to the party every penny we make above what is absolutely necessary to keep us alive.
>
> We Communists don't have the time or the money for many movies, or concerts, or T-bone steaks, or decent homes and new cars. We've been described as fanatics. We are fanatics. Our lives are dominated by one thing, the struggle for world communism.
>
> We Communists have a philosophy of life which no amount of money could buy. We have a cause to fight for, a definite purpose in life. We subordinate our petty personal selves into a

great movement of humanity, and if our personal selves seem to suffer, our personal lives seem hard, or our egos appear to suffer through subordination to the Party, then we are adequately compensated by the thought that each of us in his small way is contributing to mankind something that is new and true and better for him.

There is one thing in which I am in dead earnest, and that is the communist cause. It is my life, my business, my religion, my hobby, my sweetheart, my wife and my mistress, my bread and meat. I work at it in the daytime and dream of it at night. Its hold on me grows, not lessens, as time goes by. Therefore I cannot carry on a friendship, a love affair, or even a conversation without relating to this force which both drives and guides my life. I evaluate people, books, ideas and actions according to how they affect the communist cause and by their attitude toward it. I've already been in jail because of my ideas and if necessary, I'm ready to go to the firing squad.

APPLICATION

Christians need the same level of commitment that communists have had to spread communism.

ADDITIONAL SCRIPTURES

Acts 4:13-20; 2 Corinthians 4:8-18; Ephesians 6:19,20; Philippians 1:20,21

Who Could Be More Important than the President?

KEY VERSE

"'No one who puts his hand to the plow and looks back is fit for service in the kingdom of God.'" Luke 9:62

There was a woman in one of the churches of Memphis named Pauline Port. This dear woman had a compassion for people, and her heart was especially warmed when she was around those who could not read or write. When she was 88 years old, she became involved with Frank Laubach's ministry in teaching people to read and showing compassion to the illiterate. However, she became involved with the literacy program in a significant way.

She not only had compassion for the illiterate, but she had compassion for people who were down and out. She also had a genuine love for those who were not committed to Christ and for those who were outside the Church. With her radiant faith, Pauline would lead people to Christ.

President Bush recognized her as one of the recipients of his "Points of Light" program awards. It was a special recognition for those who rendered extraordinary humanitarian services. The President came to Memphis, and he planned to have lunch with Pauline so he could present the honor.

President Bush made special arrangements to be in Tennessee, and he extended the invitation to Pauline to join him for lunch. Do you know what Pauline did? This little woman told President Bush how sorry she was, but

she would be unable to have lunch with him on that day because that was the day she went down to the state prison in Parchmen, Mississippi to visit the prisoners and share God's love with them.

She had already made that commitment and that was the most important thing in the world to her.

When you make a commitment to Christ, you should never let anything come between you and that commitment.

Psalm 31:23; 37:28; Ecclesiastes 5:4,7; Isaiah 61:1; Matthew 5:37; James 2:1-4,8,9

God, Forgive Me When I Whine

KEY VERSE

"Give thanks in all circumstances, for this is God's will for you in Christ Jesus." 1 Thessalonians 5:18

Today upon the bus I saw a lovely maiden with golden
  hair;
I envied her because she looked so fine and wished I was
  as fair.
And suddenly as she rose to leave
I watched her hobble down the aisle.
She had one leg and wore a brace, but as she passed, a
  smile.
O God, forgive me when I whine. I've got two legs,
The world is mine.

And then I stopped to buy some sweets,
The boy who sold them was so fine.
I talked with him, and he said to me,
"You know, it's good to talk with folks like you.
You see," he said, "I'm blind."
O God, forgive me when I whine. I have two eyes,
The world is mine.

Then walking down the street
I saw a lad with eyes of blue.
He stood and watched the others play
But seemed he did not know what to do.

So I watched him for a moment and then I said:
"Hey, don't you know the others here?"
He looked ahead without a word and then I knew he
  could not hear.
O God, forgive me when I whine. I have two ears,
The world is mine.

With feet to take me where I go,
With eyes to see the sunset glow,
With ears to hear what I need to know,
O God, forgive me when I whine.
I'm blessed indeed, the world is mine.

APPLICATION

Rather than looking at what you don't have, you need to thank God for all you do have.

ADDITIONAL SCRIPTURES

1 Chronicles 16:34; Philippians 4:6,11,12;
Colossians 3:15-17; 1 Thessalonians 5:16-18;
1 Timothy 6:8; James 1:2-4

Who Changed the Price Tags?

KEY VERSE

"'For where your treasure is, there your heart will be also.'" Matthew 6:21

Big Savings!

The story is told of two young people who, as a prank, broke into a department store one night. They didn't steal or destroy anything. They simply switched the price tags on everything. You can imagine the chaos when the store opened the next day and the customers found diamond rings selling for $10, shaving cream for $300, an original Hummel figurine for $2, a pocket calculator for $500, umbrellas for $1000 and gold necklaces for $5.

APPLICATION

It is easy to get the price tags in life mixed up and to put too much importance on things and too little importance on your relationship with Christ.

ADDITIONAL SCRIPTURES

Proverbs 23:4,5; Matthew 6:19-21,33; Luke 12:32-34; Ephesians 4:17-24; Colossians 2:6-10; 3:1,2; 1 Timothy 6:6-10,17-19; Hebrews 13:5; 1 John 2:15-17

Is Anybody Else Up There?

KEY VERSE

"We live by faith, not by sight." 2 Corinthians 5:7

One day a man was walking close to a steep cliff when he lost his footing and plunged over the side. As he was falling he was caught on a tree that was sticking out about half way down the cliff. He managed to get untangled and found himself hanging from a weak limb with both hands. He looked up and he saw that the cliff was almost perfectly straight and he was a long way from the top. He looked down and it was a long, long way down to the rocky bottom.

At this point the man decided that it was time to pray. He didn't pray a long, wordy prayer, he simply yelled out, "God, if You're there, help me!"

About that time he heard a voice coming from high up above that said, "I'm here My son, have no fear."

The man was a little startled at first by God's voice, but he pleaded, "Can You help me? Can You help me?"

God replied, "Yes, I can My son, but you have to have faith. Do you trust Me?"

The man answered, "Yes Lord, I trust You."

God said, "Do you really trust Me?"

The man, straining to hold on replied, "Yes Lord, I really trust You."

Then God said, "This is what I want you to do. Let go of the limb, trust Me and everything will be all right."

The man looked down at the rocks below, then he looked up at the steep cliff above him and yelled, "Is there anybody else up there?"

APPLICATION

There are times when you have to take a giant step of faith, let go and let God take over, even when the outcome is unknown.

ADDITIONAL SCRIPTURES

Psalm 18:1-6; Isaiah 12:2; Matthew 8:23-27; 17:20; Mark 6:4-6; John 14:12-14; Hebrews 11; James 2:14,17,18

"I Believe"

KEY VERSE

"Now faith is being sure of what we hope for and certain of what we do not see." Hebrews 11:1

On June 30, 1858, Charles Blondin, arguably one of the best tightrope walkers of all time, stretched a tightrope across Niagara Falls. People came by train from Buffalo, New York and Toronto, Canada to see him walk across the tightrope that was suspended high above the raging falls.

As he stepped onto the tightrope, a hush fell over the crowd. He carried with him a 40-foot-long balance bar that weighed 39 pounds. When he finally stepped foot on the Canadian side, a huge cheer arose from the crowd. Then they began to shout in unison, "Blondin, Blondin, Blondin..." Finally Blondin held up his hand asking for the crowd's attention. He asked the crowd, "How many of you believe I can put someone on my shoulders and walk across?"

First one person shouted, "I believe" and then a second and a third, until finally the whole crowd was shouting, "We believe! We believe! We believe!"

Then Blondin shouted, "Who would like to be that someone?" All of a sudden everyone got quiet. They all said they believed, but no one was willing to risk their lives.

Blondin pointed his finger first at one person and then another and asked, "Would you like to get on my back as I go across?"

They all said, "No!" until he came to Mr. McDougle, his manager, who said, "Yes."

McDougle got on Blondin's back, and a deathly silence

fell over the crowd as Blondin stepped out onto the tight rope. Carefully, step by step, Blondin made his way across. When they were about halfway across, all of a sudden the rope started swaying violently back and forth. A gambler, who had bet Blondin would not make it, had cut the guy wire that held the rope in place.

Blondin stopped right in the middle and got McDougle down off his back temporarily to talk to him. Blondin looked at McDougle and said, "If we are going to make it safely to the other side, you can no longer be McDougle. You have to become a part of me. You can do nothing to try to balance yourself; you have to let me do everything. If you do anything on your own, we will both die. McDougle then got back on Blondin's shoulders and Blondin began to walk and then he began to run down the rope to safety on the other side.

APPLICATION

Faith is more than just a belief in your mind. It is a conviction in your heart that causes you to take action.

ADDITIONAL SCRIPTURES

Psalm 18; Isaiah 12:2; Matthew 8:23-26; 14:22-32; 17:20; John 14:12; 2 Corinthians 4:18; Galatians 3:11-14; Hebrews 11:1-39; James 2:14-26

The Forty Martyrs of Sebaste

KEY VERSE

"Here is a trustworthy saying: If we died with him, we will also live with him." 2 Timothy 2:11

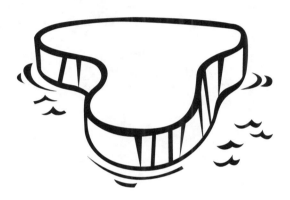

There were once forty soldiers, all Christians who were members of the famed Twelfth Legion of Rome's imperial army. One day their captain told them Emperor Licinius had sent out an edict that all soldiers were to offer sacrifice to the pagan gods. The Christians replied, "You can have our armor and even our bodies, but our hearts' allegiance belongs to Jesus Christ."

It was midwinter of A.D. 320, and the captain had them marched onto a nearby frozen lake. He stripped them of their clothes and said they would either die or renounce Christ. Throughout the night these men huddled together singing their song, "Forty Martyrs for Christ." One by one the temperature took its toll and they fell to the ice.

At last there was only one man left. He lost courage and stumbled to shore, where he renounced Christ. The officer of the guards had been watching all this. Unknown to the others, he had secretly come to believe in Christ. When he saw this last man break rank, he walked out onto the ice, threw off his clothes, and confessed that he also was a Christian. When the sun rose the next morning, there were forty bodies of soldiers who had fought to the death for Christ.

APPLICATION

If you willingly stand for Christ, even when threatened with death, you can be assured that one day you will live and reign with Him.

ADDITIONAL SCRIPTURES

Daniel 3; Acts 7:54—8:3; Philippians 1:20,21;
2 Thessalonians 1:4-10; 2 Timothy 2:11-13; 4:1-8;
Hebrews 11:32-40; James 1:12; 1 Peter 3:14;
Revelation 12:10,11

The Benefits of Suffering

KEY VERSES

"We rejoice in our sufferings, because we know that suffering produces perseverance; perseverance, character; and character, hope." Romans 5:3,4

SPECIAL

A man confined to bed because of a lingering illness saw a cocoon of a beautiful species of butterfly on his windowsill. As nature took its course, the butterfly began its struggle to emerge from the cocoon. But it was a long, hard battle. As the hours went by the struggling insect seemed to make almost no progress. Finally the man took a pair of scissors and snipped the opening a little larger to help the butterfly. Then the butterfly crawled out, but all it ever did was crawl! The stress of the struggle was intended to push colorful, life-giving juices back into the wings, but because the man cut this process short, the butterfly who was meant to fly on rainbow wings through the sky was condemned to spend its brief life crawling in the dust.

Our Relationship with God

Suffering

APPLICATION

Although you would sometimes like to skip the times of struggle and suffering in your life, it is through these times that your faith is strengthened.

ADDITIONAL SCRIPTURES

Romans 5:3-5; 2 Timothy 4:5-8; Hebrews 10:32-36; 12:1,2,10; James 1:2-4,12; 2 Peter 1:5-8; Revelation 2:19

The Charlie Lubin Story

KEY VERSE

"Let us not become weary in doing good, for at the proper time we will reap a harvest if we do not give up." Galatians 6:9

Charlie Lubin made great cheesecake. In fact, it was so good that he decided to open a cheesecake store, which he did on the north side of Chicago. It went so well that he opened a second store in South Chicago. That store did not do so well and eventually he lost both stores as a result.

He sat in his room one night and while eating his cheesecake, thought *This is good cheesecake!* So he eventually opened his original store again. After a while he opened another store which did not do so well and he once again lost both stores.

A few months later, while eating his cheesecake he said to himself, *This is good cheesecake!* And so he opened his original store again. But, after opening a second store, he went bankrupt again. This happened a fourth time!

Months later, Charlie sat in his house eating his cheesecake and thought to himself again, *This is good cheesecake!* And so he decided to open another store again! Only this time, he would name his cheesecakes after his daughter, Sara Lee. It became the largest bakery in the world!

APPLICATION

Perseverance is honored by the Lord.

ADDITIONAL SCRIPTURES

Romans 5:1-5; 1 Corinthians 15:58; 2 Corinthians 4:1;
Hebrews 12:1-3; James 1:2-4,12; 2 Peter 1:5-8

Do unto Others As You Would Have Them Do unto You

KEY VERSES

"Do not be deceived: God cannot be mocked. A man reaps what he sows. The one who sows to please his sinful nature, from that nature will reap destruction; the one who sows to please the Spirit, from the Spirit will reap eternal life."
Galatians 6:7,8

A hardworking carpenter was put in charge of building a very nice house for the general contractor he worked for. His boss gave him full responsibility for the construction project. He was supposed to order all the materials, hire all the subcontractors and supervise every aspect of the construction. The plans called for the finest materials and the most skilled laborers.

But as the carpenter began to think about the years he had worked for his boss and how little he had gotten in return, he decided to use this as an opportunity to make some money for himself. So instead of buying the best materials, he bought poor quality materials and pocketed the difference in price. Rather than hiring the most skilled workmen available, he hired the cheapest workmen he could find.

When the house was finally completed, it contained second-grade lumber, poorly poured concrete, cheap wiring and cut-rate plumbing fixtures. The day the house was finished, his boss called him into his office. He told him how much he appreciated his hard work and

dedication over the years. He said he had been planning to do something to show his appreciation for many months. Then he held out the keys to the house that had just been completed and said, "You have been such a dedicated, faithful employee for all these years that I have decided to reward you by giving you as a gift this very house which you have built."

APPLICATION

Don't try to cut corners in your life, believing that no one will know and that it won't make a difference. In the end you will reap what you have sown.

ADDITIONAL SCRIPTURES

Hosea 10:12,13; Matthew 7:12 (also Luke 6:31); Matthew 10:26; Romans 1:1-11; 2 Corinthians 9:6; Colossians 3:23,24

Work Attitudes

Your King

KEY VERSE

"So whether you eat or drink or whatever you do, do it all for the glory of God." 1 Corinthians 10:31

Long ago, a band of minstrels lived in a faraway land. They traveled from town to town singing and playing their music in hopes of making a living. They had not been doing well financially, however. Times were hard and the common people had little money to spend on concerts, even though their fee was small.

The group met one evening to discuss their plight. "I see no reason for opening tonight," one said. "It's snowing and no one will come out on a night like this."

Another said, "I agree. Last night we performed for just a handful. Even fewer will come tonight."

The leader of the troupe responded, "I know you are discouraged. I am too, but we have a responsibility to those who might come. We will go on, and we will do the best job that we are capable of doing. It is not the fault of those who come that others do not. They should not be punished with less than our best."

Heartened by his words, the minstrels gave their best performance ever. After the show, the old man called his troupe to him again. In his hand was a note, handed to him by one of the audience members just before the doors closed behind him. Slowly the man read, "Thank you for a beautiful performance." It was signed simply, "Your King."[3]

APPLICATION

Everything you do should be done as if God Himself were the benefactor of your efforts.

ADDITIONAL SCRIPTURES

Matthew 25:34-45; Colossians 3:17; 1 Peter 4:10,11

Note:
3. *God's Little Devotional Book for Students* (Tulsa, Okla.: Honor Books, 1995), p. 45.

Only the Applause of God

KEY VERSES

"Whatever you do, work at it with all your heart, as working for the Lord, not for men, since you know that you will receive an inheritance from the Lord as a reward." Colossians 3:23,24

There was once a great pianist who was giving a concert in a large concert hall. When he finished the concert, everyone in the place stood up and gave him a standing ovation. Well, almost everyone. There was one old man in the front row who didn't stand, but everyone else was on their feet cheering wildly.

When the pianist walked off the stage, he was crying. His manager asked him what was wrong and he said, "Didn't you see the man in the first row who wasn't standing and wasn't applauding?"

The manager said, "Sure, I saw him. But that was the only person who was not standing and cheering. Why worry about one old man?"

Then the pianist said, "But you don't understand. That man was the composer of the music that I played tonight. He is the only one who counts. He is the only one who knows what the piece is supposed to sound like."

APPLICATION

Many hunger for the cheers of the crowd when they actually need to be listening for only the applause of God. If God says, "Well done," it doesn't matter what the rest of the world says.

ADDITIONAL SCRIPTURES

Matthew 3:17; 6:33; 24:45-47; 25:14-30; John 5:30; 1 Corinthians 3:10-15; 2 Corinthians 5:9; Galatians 1:10; 6:8; 1 Thessalonians 4:1; 2 Timothy 2:3,4

Keeping Up Your Guard

KEY VERSE

"So, if you think you are standing firm, be careful that you don't fall!" 1 Corinthians 10:12

Lane Adams, a member of Billy Graham's staff, was a fighter pilot in World War II. He tells the story of a particular island of extreme importance to the Allied success in the South Pacific. This island was held by the Japanese and was very well fortified.

The U.S. Marine amphibious troops, supported by the U.S. air attacks, stormed the beaches and established a small foothold on the island. They only moved in about 100 feet, but it cost many, many lives. For three days they were under constant fire. They had no sleep or supplies.

Finally they were able to get supplies, and they continued to advance until they had captured almost all the island. There was only a small group of the Japanese left on one edge of the island.

Things got a lot better for the soldiers. More food and supplies were brought in. They even had chocolate to eat. They set up volleyball nets and showed movies at night.

When everything seemed to be going great, the Japanese came, it seemed like, from nowhere, and nearly drove the U.S. forces back into the sea.

APPLICATION

Never become too confident or complacent about your walk with Christ because when you think you are nearing your goal is when you can fall the easiest.

ADDITIONAL SCRIPTURES

Psalm 37:23,24; 55:22; 66:8,9; Proverbs 3:5,6; 16:18; Ephesians 6:10-18; 1 Peter 5:8,9

Prisoner of Sinful Desires

KEY VERSE

"'If the Son sets you free, you will be free indeed.'"
John 8:36

Raynald III was a fourteenth-century duke in what is now Belgium. He was grossly overweight, and he was captured by his younger brother during a revolt. His brother imprisoned him in a room that was built around him. The room had no bars on the windows, and no lock on the door. The only problem was that the door was slightly smaller than normal size and so, due to his size, Raynald III could not squeeze through the opening and set himself free.

Yet there was still hope. If he could lose enough weight, he could go free. Not only could he go free, but his brother offered to restore his title and all his wealth as soon as he left the room.

The reason the younger brother made this offer was because he knew his brother's weakness. Raynald loved to eat more than anything in the world. Each day the younger brother had a variety of delicious foods sent to Raynald's room. You can guess what happened. Instead of growing thinner, he grew fatter. He was a prisoner not of locks, bars or iron gates, but of his own appetite.

APPLICATION

Everyone is free to sin, but when you do you become a slave to sin. Christ will set you free from sin if you turn to Him.

ADDITIONAL SCRIPTURES

John 8:31-36; Romans 6:2-18; Galatians 5:1,16-21; 1 John 3:8-10

Forgetting the Basics

KEY VERSES

"We want each of you to show this same diligence to the very end, in order to make your hope sure. We do not want you to become lazy, but to imitate those who through faith and patience inherit what has been promised." Hebrews 6:11,12

A young man by the name of Ivan McGuire died not long ago at the age of 35. His death at an early age was not due to an automobile accident or a terminal illness. He wasn't murdered and he didn't commit suicide.

He was a sky diver, and he forgot to put on his parachute before jumping out of an airplane. McGuire, who aspired to be the greatest sky-diving photographer in the country, was so excited over filming some other sky divers that he failed to put on his parachute. The veteran of over 800 jumps wasn't as careful as a novice would be to check and recheck all of his equipment.

APPLICATION

You need to guard against getting overconfident in your walk with Christ. Remember to stand firm in faith through prayer, Bible study and Christian fellowship.

ADDITIONAL SCRIPTURES

Psalm 5:5; Romans 11:19-21; 1 Corinthians 10:12,13; 2 Corinthians 1:24; 1 Peter 5:5-9

The Change Sin Can Bring

KEY VERSE

"Do not be deceived: God cannot be mocked. A man reaps what he sows." Galatians 6:7

When Leonardo da Vinci was working on *The Last Supper*, he asked a young man named Pietri Bandinelli, who was a chorister in the Milan Cathedral, to sit for the character of Christ. Da Vinci spent the next twenty-five years working on the painting. He finally had only one character left to paint—Judas Iscariot. After searching and searching for the right person to sit for the character of Judas, the great artist noticed a man in the streets of Rome who he asked to be his model. His shoulders were bent toward the ground. He had a cold, hard, evil look on his face. He looked just like da Vinci's conception of Judas.

When the man was brought into Leonardo da Vinci's studio he began to look around, as if he were recalling incidents of years gone by. Finally, he turned and with a look of sad discovery he said, "Maestro, I was in this studio twenty-five years ago. I then sat for Christ."

 **APPLICATION**

You cannot sin and rebel against God without paying a high price.

 **ADDITIONAL SCRIPTURES**

Acts 17:28; Romans 6:23; Galatians 6:7-9;
Philippians 3:12-15; James 2:14-26

Praying for God's Guidance

KEY VERSE

"Do not conform any longer to the pattern of this world, but be transformed by the renewing of your mind. Then you will be able to test and approve what God's will is—his good, pleasing and perfect will." Romans 12:2

There was once an overweight guy who always stopped by a bakery on his way to work in the morning to pick up some goodies for the staff coffee break. He finally decided to go on a diet. In order to avoid the temptation to eat rich sweets, he began taking a different route to work so he didn't have to go by the bakery and be tempted. The entire office staff encouraged him as he dieted.

One day, however, he had to do an errand in the neighborhood of the bakery on the way to work. As he approached the bakery he said to himself, "Maybe God wants me to stop by the bakery this morning and pick up some goodies for the office staff." So he prayed, "Lord, if you want me to stop at the bakery this morning, make a parking spot available right in front of the bakery so there is no question in my mind." And, sure enough, there it was, a parking spot, right in front of the bakery—on his sixth trip around the block.

 **APPLICATION**

When you ask God to show you His will, do not do what you want to do and rationalize it by claiming it is God's will, but rather bend your will totally to His.

ADDITIONAL SCRIPTURES

Proverbs 3:5,6; John 5:30; Romans 7:14-25; 8:13;
1 Corinthians 9:24-27; Hebrews 2:18; 4:14-16;
James 1:13-15; 1 John 5:3-5

Automatic Pilot

KEY VERSE

"Everyone who competes in the games goes into strict training. They do it to get a crown that will not last; but we do it to get a crown that will last forever." 1 Corinthians 9:25

A true story is told about a retired couple who decided that they wanted to spend some time traveling and seeing the country while they were still physically able. They cashed in all their retirement accounts and purchased one of the finest motor homes available. One day while they were traveling up the coast of California, the husband, who had been doing all the driving up until this point, became very tired so he asked his wife if she would drive while he took a nap.

As she was driving, she put the motor home in cruise control and it worked perfectly. After driving about an hour down the straight highway, she got up to go to the bathroom. She thought, or at least that is what she told the California Highway Patrol, that cruise control was the same as automatic pilot. Their motor home crashed and was completely demolished, but neither of them were seriously hurt.

APPLICATION

You can never put your life on automatic pilot. You have to constantly discipline yourself so that you won't end up going "off the road."

ADDITIONAL SCRIPTURES

Romans 11:17-20; 1 Corinthians 9:25-27; 1 Timothy 4:15,16; 2 Timothy 2:15; 4:1,2,7,8; Hebrews 12:3-11

Watch Out for Those Tadpoles

KEY VERSE

"If we confess our sins, he is faithful and just and will forgive us our sins and purify us from all unrighteousness." 1 John 1:9

The story is told of a college campus that was located in a valley between two mountains. The water tower for that college was located up on one of the mountains. One morning while the guys were taking their showers, the water went off. They thought the girls were playing a trick on them so they quickly got dressed and ran to the girls' dorm, only to find that the same thing had happened to them.

When they realized that it wasn't a trick, they called the maintenance crew. When the maintenance crew arrived, they were perplexed. They could find no pipes that were burst or valves that were turned off, so they began the tedious task of following the pipe all the way back up the mountain. Piece by piece they took it apart to see if there was any blockage. Finally, they came to the last piece of pipe that went into the water tower. They opened it, and found a big bullfrog stuck in the pipe.

They could not understand how a bullfrog could have gotten into the water tower. There was just no way. Then they realized that it hadn't come in as a big bullfrog but as a tiny tadpole. It had worked its way in and lived off the algae in the water until one day it was swimming too close and was sucked into the pipe, cutting off the water supply to the whole campus.

 **APPLICATION**

When you ignore the sin in your life, even when it is a small, seemingly insignificant thing, eventually that sin will rob you of your joy and fellowship with Christ.

 **ADDITIONAL SCRIPTURES**

Joshua 7:1-26; Psalm 32:1-5; 51:1-12; Proverbs 28:13; Micah 7:18,19; Acts 5:1-11; Hebrews 10:19-22

Our Relationships with Others

Serving Others

Changed Lives

KEY VERSE

"We loved you so much that we were delighted to share with you not only the gospel of God but our lives as well, because you had become so dear to us."
1 Thessalonians 2:8

In 1921, Lewis Lawes became the warden at Sing Sing Prison. No prison was tougher than Sing Sing during that time. But when Warden Lawes retired some 20 years later, that prison had become a humanitarian institution. Those who studied the system said credit for the change belonged to Lawes. But when he was asked about the transformation, here's what he said: "I owe it all to my wonderful wife, Catherine, who is buried outside the prison walls."

Catherine Lawes was a young mother with three small children when her husband became the warden. Everybody warned her from the beginning that she should never set foot inside the prison walls, but that didn't stop Catherine! When the first prison basketball game was held, she went—walking into the gym with her

three beautiful kids and she sat in the stands with the inmates.

Her attitude was: "My husband and I are going to take care of these men and I believe they will take care of me! I don't have to worry!"

She insisted on getting acquainted with them and their records. She discovered one convicted murderer was blind so she taught him how to read Braille. Years later, he would weep in love for her.

Later, Catherine found a deaf-mute in prison. She went to school to learn how to use sign language. Many said that Catherine Lawes was the body of Jesus that came alive again in Sing Sing from 1921 to 1937.

Then, she was killed in a car accident. The next morning Lewis Lawes didn't come to work, so the acting warden took his place. It seemed almost instantly that the prison knew something was wrong.

The following day, her body was resting in a casket in her home, three-quarters of a mile from the prison. As the acting warden took his early morning walk he was shocked to see a large crowd of the toughest, hardest-looking criminals gathered like a herd of animals at the main gate. He came closer and noted tears of grief and sadness. He knew how much they loved Catherine. He turned and faced the men, "All right, men you can go. Just be sure and check in tonight!" Then he opened the gates and a parade of criminals walked, without a guard, the three-quarters of a mile to stand in line to pay their final respects to Catherine Lawes. And every one of them checked back in. Every one!

In order to be Christ's hands and feet in the world, you need to be willing not only to *talk* about God's love but also *demonstrate* His love.

Matthew 5:14-16; 25:34-40; Hebrews 13:3; James 2:14-17; 1 John 3:16-18

Valentine's Day

KEY VERSE

"In everything I did, I showed you that by this kind of hard work we must help the weak, remembering the words the Lord Jesus himself said: 'It is more blessed to give than receive.'" Acts 20:35

A third-grade boy had spent all night preparing for Valentine's Day by making everyone in his class a card. All night he labored over the project. "One for Jenny, one for Mark," he said as he signed and sealed each one. It was a beautiful act of kindness for anyone, let alone a third-grade young man.

As he went to bed that night, the excitement of the following day caused him to toss and turn for a while. Finally he settled his thoughts. *It will be Valentine's Day soon,* he thought to himself as he drifted off to sleep.

The next day he ran to his classroom and began placing the cards he had made into the other children's special envelopes. He noticed that his was empty, but paid no attention because he would check again after the first class was finished. Again he checked and—nothing. Lunch time rolled around and still no Valentine cards—not a single one was in the little boy's envelope. "Maybe they just forgot!" he said out loud to himself.

When his mother picked him up from school, he walked to the car with his head down, looking at his feet. She noticed his Valentine's envelope was empty. He

mumbled, "Not a single one, not a single one." When he got in the car, he again mumbled, "Not a single one." He raised his fingers one by one as if counting and said, "Not a single one." He then looked at his mother and began to smile and said, "I didn't forget a single one!"

To be more Christlike, you must care more about serving others than about what others should do for you!

Romans 15:2; Ephesians 5:1,2; Philippians 2:3,4; 1 John 3:18

The Right Choice

 **KEY VERSES**

"'If anyone would come after me, he must deny himself and take up his cross and follow me. For whoever wants to save his life will lose it, but whoever loses his life for me will find it.'"
Matthew 16:24,25

Sadhu Sundar Singh (1889-1929) was an Indian Christian mystic who was raised in the Sikh religion but became a follower of Christ through a vision. On one occasion he and a companion were traveling through a pass high in the Himalayan mountains. At one point they came across an injured man lying in the snow. Sundar Singh wished to stop and help the unfortunate man, but his companion refused, saying, "We shall lose our lives if we burden ourselves with him."

But Sundar Singh would not think of leaving the man to die in the ice and snow. As his companion bade him farewell, Sundar Singh lifted the poor traveler onto his back. With great exertion on his part, he bore the man onward, but gradually the heat from Sundar Singh's body began to warm up the poor frozen fellow, and he revived. Soon both were walking together side by side. Catching up with his former companion, they found him dead—frozen by the cold.

APPLICATION

When we forget ourselves and live totally for Christ, we discover the abundant life God intended for each of us.

ADDITIONAL SCRIPTURES

Matthew 10:37-39; 22:34-40; 25:31-46;
Luke 9:23-27; 10:25-37; John 12:25

After All He Has Done for Me

KEY VERSE

"'Greater love has no one than this, that he lay down his life for his friends.'" John 15:13

One day a man was traveling by train from Washington, D.C. to Miami, Florida. The train had just left the station when he noticed a strange occurrence. Just a few seats in front of him a gentleman began to have a rather severe seizure which threw him sprawling to the floor. Immediately, the person seated next to him jumped up and began to help him. He held the convulsing man's head so that he wouldn't bang it on the floor, he moved him so he wouldn't hit any of the nearby seats and he continually spoke words of encouragement and comfort.

When the seizure stopped, the man gently picked up his friend and set him back in his seat and applied a cool, moist cloth to his forehead. Soon, they were both asleep.

The scene repeated itself several times before they had arrived in Miami.

Upon arrival, the man who had been observing all of this approached the helping friend and asked him: "Can you please tell me the story behind your friend with the seizures?" The gentleman was happy to reply and told this story:

"Several years ago my friend and I were in Vietnam. We had both been wounded, but only I couldn't walk. My friend stayed with me behind enemy lines. Finally, after three days he picked me up and carried me back to an American camp. That trip took three weeks and we should have been killed. We were soon shipped home

and became separated. A few years later I learned that my friend was having these seizures due to his injury. Of course, my leg had healed completely. He was alone, and desperate and completely unable to help himself. I quit my job, sold everything I had and went to help him. I figured after all he'd done for me, there wasn't anything I wouldn't do for him."

Because Christ willingly gave His life for you, you need to be willing to give up everything for Him.

Matthew 19:16-30; 22:37-39; Romans 5:6-8;
1 Thessalonians 2:8; 1 John 3:16

A Lesson in Servanthood

KEY VERSE

"'Whoever wants to become great among you must be your servant, and whoever wants to be first must be the slave of all.'" Mark 10:43,44

Thirty-five high school students were helping lead a camp for handicapped people of all ages and with every kind of disability. During the event, they had a birthday party for Jesus. As part of the birthday celebration they had confetti, noisemakers and the typical party fare. Each camper and his or her partner took turns throwing confetti, popping balloons and blowing noisemakers. A good time was had by all.

At the end of the evening, to help expedite cleanup, the youth leader challenged everyone to squat down where they were and pick up a handful of confetti or balloons or whatever and make at least one trip to the trash can before leaving. What happened next was a wonder.

One of the campers who was blind and in her late teens was crawling around on the floor feeling for handfuls of trash, handing it to her partner for proper disposal and then crawling for more.

The youth leader felt a sense of awe at this selfless and unexpected act of service on the girl's part, but he said he also felt shame at his own desire to give out the instructions but not participate in the cleanup.

True greatness is not found in the power a leader exerts but in his or her willingness to become a servant.

Matthew 20:25-28 (also Mark 10:42-45; Luke 22:25-27); Matthew 23:11,12; Luke 9:48; 17:7-10; John 13:1-17; Galatians 5:13,14; Philippians 2:6,7

Not Everyone Is Blind

KEY VERSE

"Each of you should look not only to your own interests, but also to the interests of others."
Philippians 2:4

In his book, *Lord, It Has Been One of Those Days*, Bob Brown tells of a pastor who visited an elderly blind lady who was a member of his church. It was during the Christmas season, and he noticed that the Christmas tree in her house was brightly decorated with lights and ornaments.

He said to her, "Do you do this every year?"

"Yes," she replied, "this is one of the big things I do. I always look forward to it. My nephew always goes out and gets a Christmas tree, then together we get the Christmas decorations out and decorate the tree."

The pastor thought to himself, *A blind woman with a brightly lighted Christmas tree?*

He then indicated to her that he did not want to be offensive, but he could not quite understand why a blind woman would want to have a brightly decorated tree and lights in the window.

The dear little lady tilted her head towards him and said, "Pastor, everybody is not blind."

_____ **APPLICATION**

Christians should desire to make others happy as well as themselves.

_____ **ADDITIONAL SCRIPTURES**

Matthew 22:38; Romans 15:1,2; 1 Corinthians 10:24,31-33; 13:4,5; Galatians 6:10

Whose Duty Is It?

KEY VERSE

"Command them to do good, to be rich in good deeds, and to be generous and willing to share. In this way they will lay up treasure for themselves as a firm foundation for the coming age, so that they may take hold of the life that is truly life."
1 Timothy 6:18,19

Some years ago there was a shipwreck off the Pacific Northwest coast. A crowd of fishermen in a nearby village gathered to watch the ship as it was smashed on the rocks. A lifeboat was sent to the rescue, and after a terrific struggle, the rescuers came back with all of the ship-wrecked sailors but one.

"There was no room in the lifeboat for him, so we told him to stay by the ship and someone would come back for him," one of the rescuers explained.

"Who will come with me?" shouted a young man from the crowd.

Just then a little old lady cried out, "Don't go, Jim, my son. Don't go. You are all I have left. Your father was drowned in the sea; your brother William sailed away and we've never heard from him; and now if you are lost, I'll be left alone. Oh, Jim, please don't go."

Jim listened patiently to his mother's pleading, then said, "Mother, I must go! It is my duty. I must go!"

The onlookers watched as the men in the lifeboat fought their way back toward the wreck. Anxiously Jim's mother wept and prayed. They saw the boat heading back to shore, a frail little shell tossed about by the waves. At last when the boat came close enough to hear, those

on shore shouted, "Did you get him?"

And Jim shouted back, "Yes, and tell Mother it's her son William!"

_____ **APPLICATION**

When you give yourself unselfishly to help others, you may be rewarded in unexpected ways.

_____ **ADDITIONAL SCRIPTURES**

Ruth 2:11,12; Matthew 10:42; Mark 4:24; Luke 6:38; Ephesians 6:6-8; Colossians 3:23,24; Hebrews 13:16; Revelation 22:12

A Few Brownies Can Go a Long Way

KEY VERSE

"Dear children, let us not love with words or tongue but with actions and in truth." 1 John 3:18

A number of years ago in a Boston mental institution there was a young girl who was locked in the dungeon. The doctors had placed "Little Annie" in a small cage that received little light because she was hopelessly insane. At times Annie would violently attack people who came into her cage. At other times she would just ignore them. She was destined to spend her whole life in this dreadful place.

There was a retired nurse who lived nearby and she felt there was hope for any child, so she started visiting the dungeon and trying to communicate some love and hope to the little girl in the cage. When the nurse first started visiting Annie, she acted as if she were not aware of the nurse's presence.

One day the nurse brought some brownies to the dungeon and left them within reach just outside the cage. Little Annie did not respond, but when the nurse returned the next day, the brownies were gone. Every Thursday after that when the nurse would visit, she would bring brownies and leave them for Annie. Soon after that the doctors began to notice a dramatic change taking place. They decided to move Annie upstairs. Finally she was released and told that she could go home, but Little Annie didn't leave. She chose instead to stay and help others.

Little Annie's full name was Anne Sullivan, and one day she had the opportunity to care for and teach Helen Keller how to communicate with the world she could neither see nor hear.

It is easy to say you love those in need. It is far more difficult to put those words into action.

Ezekiel 33:30,31; Matthew 5:43-47;
1 Corinthians 13:1-8; 1 Peter 4:8-10; 1 John 3:16-18

How to Make a Difference

KEY VERSE

"There are different kinds of gifts, but the same Spirit. There are different kinds of service, but the same Lord. There are different kinds of working, but the same God works all of them in all men." 1 Corinthians 12:4-6

A young boy wrote a letter to Mother Teresa. He asked her how he could make a difference with his life, like she had with hers. For months he didn't hear anything from her. Then one day he received a letter from Calcutta, India. He expectantly opened it up and read four words that changed his life.

"Find your own Calcutta."

Mother Teresa

_____ **APPLICATION**

We all have to find our own Calcutta. Where is your Calcutta? Your friends? Your school? Your family?

_____ **ADDITIONAL SCRIPTURES**

Matthew 9:36-38; 25:31-46; Mark 10:45; Luke 9:23; John 20:21; Acts 1:8; Romans 12:4-8; Ephesians 4:16

Good News

KEY VERSE

"For the love of money is a root of all kinds of evil. Some people, eager for money, have wandered from the faith and pierced themselves with many griefs."
1 Timothy 6:10

Robert De Vincenzo, the great Argentine golfer, once won a tournament. After receiving the check and smiling for the cameras, he went to the clubhouse and prepared to leave. Later, as he walked alone to his car in the parking lot, he was approached by a young woman. She congratulated him on his victory, then told him that her child was seriously ill and near death. She did not know how she could pay the doctor's bills and hospital expenses.

De Vincenzo was touched by her story, and he took out a pen and endorsed his winning check for payment to the woman. "Make some good days for your baby," he said as he pressed the check into her hand.

The next week he was having lunch at a country club when a PGA official came to his table. "Some of the boys in the parking lot last week told me you met a young woman there after you won that tournament."

De Vincenzo nodded. "Well," said the official, "I have news for you. She's a phony. She has no sick baby. She's not even married. She fleeced you, my friend."

"You mean there is no baby who is dying?" said De Vincenzo.

"That's right," said the official.

"That's the best news I've heard all week," De Vincenzo said.

APPLICATION

Christians must be more concerned with the welfare of others than with their time, possessions or money.

ADDITIONAL SCRIPTURES

Matthew 6:24,33; Luke 16:13; 1 Timothy 6:6-10;
2 Timothy 3:1-5; Titus 1:7,8; Hebrews 13:5;
1 Peter 5:2,3

The Praying Hands

The famous *Praying Hands* picture was created by Albert Dürer, who was born in Germany in 1471, the son of a Hungarian goldsmith. While Albert was studying art, he and a friend roomed together. The meager income that they earned on the side as they studied did not meet their living expenses. Albert suggested that he would go to work to earn the necessary income for both of them while his friend pursued his studies. When finished, the friend would then go to work to provide support while Albert continued his studies. The friend liked the plan, but insisted that he be the first to work so Albert could continue his studies.

Albert became a skilled artist and engraver. After selling a wood engraving one day, Albert announced that he was ready to begin supporting his friend as he studied. But because of all the hard menial labor, his friend's hands were so swollen that he was no longer able to hold a brush, yet alone use it with skill. His career as an artist was ended.

Albert was deeply saddened by his friend's suffering. One day when he returned to their room, he heard his friend praying and saw his hands held in a reverent attitude of prayer. At that moment, Albert was inspired to create the picture of those praying hands. His friend's lost skill could never be restored, but through this picture

Albert Dürer felt that he could express his love and appreciation for his friend's self-sacrifice. He hoped that such a picture could inspire others to appreciate similar acts of self-sacrifice that they had received from family and friends.

The selfless deeds done for others may never receive public attention, but they will often have an eternal impact.

Ruth 1:16,17; Psalm 133:1; Micah 6:8; Romans 12:10; 1 John 3:16-19; Philippians 2:3,4

A Lesson in Giving

KEY VERSE

"A generous man will prosper; he who refreshes others will himself be refreshed." Proverbs 11:25

A group of students from the Midwest took a trip to the dump in Tijuana, Mexico to minister Christ's love. During the trip, they saw large numbers of families living in makeshift hovels made of cardboard, scrap tin, and other bits of refuse.

There were several small boys about 10 years of age playing and wrestling nearby. These boys appeared to own only the clothes and shoes that they were wearing, and these were not in the best condition. Although they were seemingly happy and carefree, they were quite dirty and obviously not involved in school.

The bravest of the three boys approached the youth leader and tried to make conversation. The boy's English was not very good and the youth leader's Spanish was nil. However, they did the best they could to communicate by adding hand signals to their interaction.

Then the youth leader reached into his pocket and took out a piece of gum to share with him. What happen next brought tears to the eyes of the leader. The boy took that one piece of gum, tore it into three pieces and ran and shared it with his two friends. You would have thought he had just been given the greatest gift—much more than a small bit of gum.

The youth leader said if he had been that young boy, he no doubt could have quickly put the entire piece in his mouth and counted his good fortune. But, thankfully,

God taught him a lesson about giving from a young boy who had very little to give.

APPLICATION

Sometimes those who have the least to give are the most generous. They will reap the benefits of their generosity.

ADDITIONAL SCRIPTURES

Luke 6:38; 21:1-4; Acts 2:44-47; 20:35; 2 Corinthians 8:1-15; 9:6-15; Philippians 4:14-19; 1 Timothy 6:18,19

Give and It Will Be Given to You

KEY VERSE

"'Give, and it will be given to you. A good measure, pressed down, shaken together and running over, will be poured into your lap. For with the measure you use, it will be measured to you.'" Luke 6:38

Two young men who were working their way through Leland Stanford University found themselves low on funds. The idea came to one of them to engage Ignacy Paderewski, the famous Polish pianist, composer and statesman, for a piano recital and use their profits to meet their expenses.

The pianist's manager asked for a guarantee of $2,000. The boys staged the concert, but the proceeds totaled only $1,600. Humiliated, the boys sought out the great artist and told him of their efforts. They gave him the entire $1,600 and a promissory note for the remaining $400, explaining that they would earn the amount at the earliest possible moment.

"No boys, that won't do," he told them. Tearing up the note, he returned the money to them and said, "Now take all of your expenses out of the $1,600 and each of you keep 10 percent for the balance for your work. Let me have the rest."

The years rolled by. The war came and Paderewski was striving with all his means to feed thousands of starving Poles. There was only one man in the entire world who could help him.

Thousands of tons of food began to enter Poland for distribution by the premier. After the starving people were fed, Paderewski journeyed to Paris to thank the

president of the United States, Herbert Hoover, for the relief sent to his country.

"That's all right, Mr. Paderewski," was Hoover's reply. "You don't remember, but you helped me once when I was a struggling college student and I was in the hole."

Always treat other people the way you want to be treated because you never know when the tables will be turned.

Matthew 7:12; 25:34-40; Luke 6:31-38; Romans 13:8-10; 2 Corinthians 9:6-8; Galatians 5:14,15; Hebrews 13:2,3

The Power of Our Words

"Therefore encourage one another and build each other up, just as in fact you are doing."
1 Thessalonians 5:11

In the country church of a small village an altar boy serving the priest at Sunday mass accidentally dropped the cruet of wine. The village priest struck the altar boy sharply on the cheek and in a gruff voice shouted, "Leave the altar and don't come back!" That boy became Tito, the communist leader.

In a cathedral of a large city an altar boy serving the bishop at Sunday mass accidentally dropped the cruet of wine. With a warm twinkle in his eyes the bishop gently whispered, "Someday you will be a priest." That boy grew up to become Archbishop Fulton Sheen, one of the greatest Christian Catholic communicators of the twentieth century.

APPLICATION

There is power in encouraging words. Far too many people hear too few encouraging words.

ADDITIONAL SCRIPTURES

Matthew 12:36,37; Romans 14:19; Ephesians 4:29; Philippians 4:8,9; Colossians 3:8; Hebrews 10:25; James 3:5-12

Being a Part
of the Body

Making the Church Together

KEY VERSE

"Those parts of the body that seem to be weaker are indispensable,...so that there should be no division in the body, but that its parts should have equal concern for each other."
1 Corinthians 12:22,25

A teacher at Vacation Bible School invited the students to join her in their usual closing ceremony. "Let's make our churches," she said. "Here's the church and here's the steeple, open the doors and there's—"

Just then it hit her. She had totally forgotten about the little boy who had joined the class that day, who was missing one arm. She had been so worried about one of the children making a comment about his handicap or saying something else to embarrass him. Now, the very thing she had worried about the children doing, she had done.

As she stood there speechless, trying to decide what to do, the most wonderful thing happened. The little girl sitting next to the boy reached over with her left hand and placed it up to his right hand and said, "Davey, let's make the church together."

APPLICATION

We all need one another. It is easy for us to see how the weak need the strong, but we also need to realize that the strong need the seemingly weaker parts to be a complete body.

ADDITIONAL SCRIPTURES

Ecclesiastes 4:9-12; Romans 15:1,2;
1 Corinthians 1:27-29; 12:12,14-26;
2 Corinthians 12:7-10

Trying to Do the Job Alone

KEY VERSE

"Let us consider how we may spur one another on toward love and good deeds. Let us not give up meeting together, as some are in the habit of doing, but let us encourage one another—and all the more as you see the Day approaching."
Hebrews 10:24,25

To: Workers' Compensation Claims Department
From: Mr. Joe Blattner
Date: September 12, 1986
Re: Workers' Comp Claim
Date of Loss: August 15, 1986

Gentlemen:

I am writing in response to your request for more information concerning Block #11 on the insurance form which asks for "the cause of injury" wherein I had written "trying to do the job alone." You indicated a need for further information, so I trust the following will be sufficient.

I am a bricklayer by trade, and on the date of injury I was working alone laying brick around the top of a four-story building when I realized that I had about 500 pounds of brick left over. Rather than carry the bricks down by hand, I decided to put them into a barrel and lower them by pulley, which was fastened to the top of the building.

I secured the end of the rope at the ground level and went up to the top of the building and loaded the bricks into the barrel. I then pushed the barrel off the top of the building, loaded with bricks. I then went down and untied the rope, holding it securely to ensure the slow descent of the barrel.

As you will note on Block #6 of the Work Comp claim form, I weigh 145 pounds. Due to my shock at being jerked

Being a Part of the Body

off the ground so swiftly, I lost my presence of mind and forgot to let go of the rope. Between the second and third floors I met the barrel coming down. This accounts for the bruises and lacerations on my upper body.

Regaining my presence of mind, again I held tightly onto the rope and proceeded rapidly up the side of the building, scraping my side as I went up. I did not stop until my right hand was jammed in the pulley. This accounts for my broken thumb.

Despite the pain, I retained my presence of mind and held tightly to the rope. At approximately the same time, however, the barrel of bricks hit the ground and the bottom fell out of the barrel. Devoid of the weight of the bricks, the barrel now weighed about 40 pounds. I again refer you to block #6 and my weight.

As you may guess, I began a rapid descent. In the vicinity of the second floor I met the barrel coming up. This explains the injuries to my legs and lower body. Slowed only slightly, I continued my descent, landing on the pile of bricks. Fortunately, my back was only sprained and the internal injuries were minimal. My ankles will heal well, I'm sure, and the break in my right foot has been x-rayed, and shows only a hairline fracture.

I am sorry to report, however, that at this point I lost my presence of mind and let go of the rope. As you may imagine the empty barrel came down upon me with a vengeance, and thus the explanation for the 235 stitches on my scalp and back. The concussion was mild, and my memory should be fine in a few days.

I trust this answers your concern re: what I meant about "trying to do the job alone." Please be well assured that in the future I will endeavor to share the workload.

APPLICATION

Christians have available to them the strength and support they gain through fellowship with other Christians, thus they should never try to do the job alone.

ADDITIONAL SCRIPTURES

Exodus 18:14-26; Proverbs 11:14; 15:22; Ecclesiastes 4:9-12; Acts 2:42-47; Romans 12:4,5; 1 Corinthians 12:12-26

Wasted Away Due to Lack of Use

KEY VERSE

"'For everyone who has will be given more, and he will have an abundance. Whoever does not have, even what he has will be taken from him.'"
Matthew 25:29

New and IMPROVED

In Sogovia, Spain, there is what remains of an aqueduct built by the victorious Romans in the year 109. For 18 centuries this aqueduct carried sparkling water from the mountains to one town.

About the turn of the century it was decided that the aqueduct should be preserved for posterity. Modern pipes were laid and the sparkling water was rerouted through these new pipes.

Shortly thereafter the aqueduct started to fall apart. The sun dried the mortar and it crumbled. Then the stones sagged and fell into ruins.

APPLICATION

When you fail to use the talents God has given you, you will lose them.

Being a Part
of the Body

Matthew 25:14-29; Mark 4:21-25; Luke 6:38; 8:16-18;
16:10; 19:11-26; 1 Corinthians 12:7-31; James 4:17;
2 Peter 1:5-9

Being a Part
of the Body

The "Bodies"

KEY
VERSE

"From him the whole body, joined and held
together by every supporting ligament, grows and
builds itself up in love, as each part does its work."
Ephesians 4:16

Once upon a time there were four people named
Everybody, Somebody, Nobody and Anybody.

When there was an important job to be done,
Everybody was sure that Somebody would do it. Anybody
could have done it, but Nobody did it.

When Nobody did it, Everybody got angry because it
was Everybody's job. Everybody thought that Somebody
would do it. But Nobody realized that Nobody would do
it.

So it ended up that Everybody blamed Somebody
when Nobody did what Anybody could have done in the
first place.

_____ APPLICATION

Everyone has a purpose within the Church—the Body of Christ. If you are not doing what God called you to do, it may not get done.

_____ ADDITIONAL SCRIPTURES

Ecclesiastes 4:9-12; Romans 12:3-8; 1 Corinthians 12:4-31; Ephesians 4:11-13

Breaking Out of Prison

KEY VERSE

> "'For if you forgive men when they sin against you, your heavenly Father will also forgive you.'"
> Matthew 6:14

The year was 1947. It was almost two full years after the liberation of Auschwitz, as Corrie ten Boom stepped forward to share the message of forgiveness and healing at a German church. As she stepped forward she prayed that God would use her words to bring about healing, forgiveness and restoration. What she was about to experience changed her life forever.

As she finished her message, a man stepped forward, moving his way through the crowd of people there to talk to Corrie. He looked familiar, like she'd seen him somewhere before. As she looked into his eyes, it all became crystal clear. She recognized him...the uniform...the whips...walking past him naked at the selection. She remembered her sister dying a slow and painful death at his hands. The memories came flooding back to her...memories from Auschwitz and this man who had been a guard at the camp.

"I'm a Christian now." He spoke with his eyes sadly looking into hers. "I know that God has forgiven me, but will *you* forgive me?" He stretched out his hand to receive hers.

She stood there for what must have seemed an eternity, although it was probably only a moment or two. She knew that she needed to make a choice. Would she forgive the man at whose hand she experienced so much hurt, pain and humiliation? Would she? Could she?

"Jesus, I need your help. I can lift my hand, but you need to supply the feeling." She slowly raised her hand, reached out to the man and took his hand in hers. As she reached out, a warm sensation filled her heart. God was indeed faithful. "I forgive you, brother—with my whole heart!"

That day, former guard and former prisoner were both healed and set free from the bondage of bitterness and anger.

It's not always easy, but forgiveness will bring freedom and healing.

Matthew 6:12,15; 18:21-35; Mark 11:25,26; Luke 6:34; Ephesians 4:31,32; Colossians 3:13; Hebrews 12:14,15

Forgiving Others

Paco

KEY VERSE

"""For this son of mine was dead and is alive again; he was lost and is found.'" So they began to celebrate.""" Luke 15:24

There is a story told about a father and his teenage son. They had a strained relationship, so much so that finally the young son ran away from home. Immediately the father began a journey across Spain in search of his rebellious young son.

Finally after months and months and months of searching he arrived in Madrid. In a last desperate effort to find his son, the father went down to the newspaper office and put an ad in the newspaper. It simply said, "Dear Paco, meet me in front of the newspaper office at noon. All is forgiven. I love you. Your father."

The next day at noon in front of the newspaper office 800 Pacos showed up all seeking forgiveness.

People everywhere are looking for the forgiveness that Christ is ready to give.

Isaiah 1:18; Psalm 32:1,2; 51:7; 103:1-13; Luke 15:11-24; Hebrews 8:12; Revelation 7:13-17

Forgiving Others

Do It Now!

KEY VERSE

"Bear with each other and forgive whatever grievances you may have against one another. Forgive as the Lord forgave you." Colossians 3:13

Hubert Humphrey was one of the twentieth century's great politicians and a political rival of Richard Nixon. At the funeral of Hubert Humphrey, Richard Nixon sat next to Humphrey's wife. The following incident tells why:

Hubert Humphrey had a terminal illness. A few days before Mr. Humphrey's death, the chaplain walked into the hospital room to visit with him. Humphrey was talking on the telephone with a man named Dick. Several times he mentioned Dick's name.

After he hung up the phone, the chaplain said, "To whom were you talking?"

He said, "To Richard Nixon." He then told him how he had called Richard Nixon to ask him to forgive him for the times he had hurt him. He shared that it was one of the most liberating experiences of his life to bring about reconciliation between him and a political adversary.

The chaplain asked, "How could you talk with him like that?"

Humphrey replied, "You, chaplain, of all folks should know."

While on the phone that day, Hubert Humphrey had asked Nixon to sit with his wife at his funeral. What a beautiful picture of forgiveness.

APPLICATION

Don't wait until you are on your deathbed to forgive the people you hold grudges against or you'll have to wait until then to experience the joy and freedom of forgiving others and being forgiven in return.

ADDITIONAL SCRIPTURES

Matthew 6:14,15; 18:21-35; Luke 6:38; Romans 12:19-21; 2 Corinthians 2:10,11; Ephesians 4:32

Our Relationships with Others

Being a Witness to Others

The Class Address

KEY VERSE

"Be joyful always." 1 Thessalonians 5:16

One day Charles Spurgeon, a famous evangelical English preacher, was addressing one of his classes. "When you speak of heaven, you should let your face become bright, happy, alive! But when you speak of hell, well…your ordinary face will do."

APPLICATION

If Christ is in our heart, our face should reflect the joy He gives us.

ADDITIONAL SCRIPTURES

Exodus 34:29-35; Psalm 5:11,12; 34:1-3; 66:1-20; 68:3;
118:24; 119:10-16; 150:1-6; Proverbs 15:13,15,30;
17:22; Habakkuk 3:18; Acts 3:1-10; Romans 5:1-5;
Philippians 4:4

Being a Witness
to Others

My Friend

KEY VERSE

"'Everyone who calls on the name of the Lord will be saved.' How, then, can they call on the one they have not believed in? And how can they believe in the one of whom they have not heard? And how can they hear without someone preaching to them?"
Romans 10:13,14

My friend, I stand in judgment now
And feel that you're to blame somehow.
On earth I walked with you by day
And never did you show the way.
You knew the Lord in truth and glory,
But never did you tell the story.
My knowledge then was very dim,
You could have led me safe to Him.
Though we lived together here on earth,
You never told me of the second birth.
And now I stand this day condemned
Because you failed to mention Him.
You taught me many things, that's true.
I called you friend and trusted you.
But I learn now that it's too late,
And you could have kept me from this fate.
We walked by day and talked by night,
And yet you showed me not the light.
You let me live and love and die,
You knew I'd never live on high.
Yes, I called you friend in life,
And trusted you throughout joy and strife
And yet on coming to this dreadful end,
I cannot now call you my friend.

Author unknown

 **APPLICATION**

There is nothing greater you can do for friends than tell them about the abundant and eternal life they can find in Christ.

 **ADDITIONAL SCRIPTURES**

Matthew 28:19,20; Acts 1:8; 1 Corinthians 15:3,4; 2 Timothy 4:2

Our
Relationships
with
Others

Being a Witness
to Others

The Strength of One Testimony

KEY VERSE

"The things you have heard me say in the presence of many witnesses entrust to reliable men who will also be qualified to teach others." 2 Timothy 2:2

Jewish physician Boris Kornfeld was imprisoned in Siberia. There he worked in surgery, helping both the staff and prisoners. He met a Christian, whose name is unknown, but whose quiet faith and frequent reciting of the Lord's Prayer moved Dr. Kornfeld.

One day while repairing the slashed artery of a guard, Dr. Kornfeld seriously considered suturing the artery in such a way that the guard would bleed to death internally over time. The violence he recognized in his own heart appalled him and he found himself saying, "Forgive us our sins as we forgive those who sin against us." Afterward, he began to refuse to obey various inhumane, immoral prison camp rules. He knew his quiet rebellion put his life in danger.

One afternoon he examined a patient who had undergone a cancer operation. He saw in the man's eyes a depth of spiritual misery that moved him, and he told him his entire story, including a confession of his secret faith. That very night, Dr. Kornfeld was murdered as he slept. Still, his testimony was not in vain. The patient who had heard his confession became, as a result, a Christian. He survived the prison camp and went on to tell the world about life in the Gulag. That patient was Aleksandr Solzhenitsyn, who became one of the great leaders of the twentieth century.[1]

APPLICATION

The Christian faith will continue to spread only as long as Christians continue to share the message of love and forgiveness to others who will in turn do the same.

ADDITIONAL SCRIPTURES

Psalm 51:10,17; Isaiah 55:11; Matthew 5:13-16; 6:9-14; 2 Timothy 1:13,14

Note:
1. *God's Little Devotional Book for Students* (Tulsa, Okla.: Honor Books, 1995), p. 81.

Being a Witness to Others

Speaking the Language

"I have become all things to all men so that by all possible means I might save some."
1 Corinthians 9:22

Many years ago in England a circus elephant named Bozo was very popular with the public. Children especially loved to crowd around his cage and throw him peanuts. Then one day there was a sudden change in the elephant's personality. Several times he tried to kill his keeper and when the children came near his cage he would charge toward them as if wanting to trample them to death. It was obvious he would have to be destroyed. The circus owner, a greedy and crude man, decided to stage a public execution of the animal and sell tickets.

The day came and the circus tent was packed. Bozo was in his cage in the center ring. A firing squad stood by with rifles. The manager stood near the cage ready to give the signal to fire when out of the crowd came a short, inconspicuous man in a brown derby hat.

"There is no need for this," he said.

But the manager brushed him aside and said, "He is a bad elephant. He must die before he kills someone."

The small man insisted, "You are wrong. Give me two minutes in the cage alone with him and I will prove you are wrong."

The manager turned and stared in amazement. "You will be killed," he said.

"I don't think so," replied the man. "Do I have your permission?"

The manager was not about to pass up such a dramatic spectacle. Even if the man were killed, the publicity alone would be worth millions. He said, "All right, but first you will have to sign a release absolving the circus of all responsibility."

The small man signed the paper. As he removed his coat

Being a Witness to Others

and hat, preparing to enter the cage, the manager told the people what was about to happen. A hush fell over the crowd. The door to the cage was unlocked, the man stepped inside, then the door was locked behind him.

At the sight of this stranger in his cage the elephant threw back his trunk, let out a mighty roar, then bent his head preparing to charge. The man stood quite still, a faint smile on his face as he began to talk to the animal. The audience was so quiet that those nearest the cage could hear the man talking but couldn't make out the words. He seemed to be speaking some foreign language.

Slowly, as the man continued to talk, the elephant raised his head. Then the crowd heard an almost piteous cry from the elephant as his enormous head began to sway gently from side to side. The man smiled and walked confidently to the animal and began to stroke the long trunk. All aggression seemed suddenly to have been drained from the elephant. Docile as a pup, he wound his trunk around the man's waist and the two walked slowly around the cage.

The astounded audience could bear the silence no longer and broke out in cheers and clapping. After a while the man bade farewell to the elephant and left the cage. He told the manager, "He'll be all right now. You see, he's an Indian elephant and none of you spoke his language, Hindustani. I would advise you to get someone around here who speaks Hindustani. He was just homesick." And with that the little man put on his coat and hat and left.

The astounded manager looked down at the slip of paper in his hand. The name the man had signed was Rudyard Kipling.

APPLICATION

If you are going to reach people with the good news of Jesus Christ, you have to learn to speak their language.

ADDITIONAL SCRIPTURES

Matthew 28:18-20; Acts 2:2-11; 1 Corinthians 9:19-22; 2 Corinthians 4:5; Revelation 7:9,10; 14:6

Being a Witness
to Others

Change Your Name

KEY VERSE

"'Let your light shine before men, that they may see your good deeds and praise your Father in heaven.'" Matthew 5:16

When Alexander the Great came out of Macedonia and Greece to conquer the Mediterranean world, on one of his campaigns he received a message that one of his soldiers was seriously misbehaving in such a way that he was hurting the reputation of all of the Greek troops. When Alexander heard about this man, he sent word that he wanted to talk to this soldier in person.

When the young man arrived at the tent of Alexander the Great, the commander asked him, "What is your name?"

The reply came back, "Alexander, sir."

Again the commander asked, "What is your name?" and again the soldier replied, "Alexander, sir."

Alexander the Great asked the soldier a third time, "What is your name?"

The soldier fearfully replied, "Alexander, sir."

The commander then looked him straight in the eyes and said forcefully, "Soldier, either change your behavior or change your name."

Being a Witness to Others

APPLICATION

If you call yourself a Christian, Christ's reputation is in your hands. Live accordingly.

ADDITIONAL SCRIPTURES

Matthew 5:14-16; John 2:12-25; Romans 2:24;
1 Corinthians 11:1; 2 Corinthians 5:20; 1 Peter 2:12

A Riddle

KEY VERSE

"'I am the way and the truth and the life. No one comes to the Father except through me.'" John 14:6

You are on the road of life and you come to a fork in the road. One road leads to heaven and the other to hell. There are two guides standing at the fork in the road, and you can ask only one question of either one of them. One of them is an absolute liar and will not tell you the truth. The other is one hundred percent honest and can only tell you the truth.

What one, and only one, question can you ask that will let you know without a doubt that you are on the right road? Even after asking this question you will not know if the guide told you the truth or not, but you will know that you have chosen the right road.

The answer: Since you can only ask one question and you don't know which guide will tell the truth, you can ask either guide this question: "If I were to ask the other guide which is the right road, what would he tell me?" You then take the opposite road.

Here is why: If it was the liar who you questioned, he will lie about the true answer the other guide will give, so you would want to take the opposite road from the one he told you. If on the other hand it was the honest guide you questioned, he will truthfully tell you the lie that the other guide would have told you. So you know the opposite road is the answer. So this one question will produce a wrong answer no matter which guide you ask and you can take the opposite road.

Being a Witness to Others

Jesus is the only truth. He doesn't try to trick us or lead us astray, He simply says, "Come."

Matthew 7:13,14; John 6:40; 8:44; 10:9,10;
Acts 4:10-12

Missed Opportunity

KEY VERSE

"The Lord is not slow in keeping his promise, as some understand slowness. He is patient with you, not wanting anyone to perish, but everyone to come to repentance." 2 Peter 3:9

One of the greatest disasters of history took place in 1271. Nichelo and Matteo Polo (the father and uncle of Marco Polo) were visiting the Kubla Kahn. Kubla Kahn at that time was a world ruler. He ruled all of China, all of India and all of the East. He was attracted to the story of Christianity as Nichelo and Matteo told it to him. And he said this to them: "You shall go to your high priest and tell him on my behalf to send me 100 men skilled in your religion, and I shall be baptized and when I am baptized all my barons and great men will be baptized and their subjects will receive baptism too and so there will be more Christians here than there are in your parts."

So Nichelo and Matteo Polo went to the highest religious authority, requesting 100 missionaries. The pope responded, "Those barbarians don't deserve the gospel."

Nothing was done for about 30 years and then only two or three missionaries were sent.

Too few. Too late.

As a result of this delay, Buddhist monks, who were pleased to come, converted the largest empire history has ever known—from China into the Middle East and Europe—to Buddhism.

APPLICATION

When you realize that you are no better than any other sinner, God is able to use you to advance His kingdom.

ADDITIONAL SCRIPTURES

Ezekiel 18:23; Matthew 28:18-20; Acts 1:8;
1 Timothy 2:1-6; Revelation 7:9,10

Dunkirk

KEY VERSE

"I tell you...there will be more rejoicing in heaven over one sinner who repents than over ninety-nine righteous persons who do not need to repent."
Luke 15:7

During the battle of Dunkirk in May of 1940, hundreds of thousands of British and French troops were trapped on the French beaches around Dunkirk.

Winston Churchill called for any seaworthy vessel to cross the English Channel to rescue the endangered troops. During six days, 328,000 troops were evacuated to safety.

The story of one lone fisherman stands out. In his 19-foot rowboat he crossed the channel, rescued two soldiers and returned to safety. He traveled to France a second time. His small engine died, but he continued rowing across and brought back two more soldiers. Then he passed out from exhaustion.

Four compared to 328,000 seems unimportant. You may say, "Big deal! Only four." However, tell that to the four men he saved from spending five years in a prison camp.

APPLICATION

You can't reach every person for Christ, but every person you reach is one less person who will have to spend eternity without Christ.

ADDITIONAL SCRIPTURES

Matthew 28:19,20; Luke 15:1-24; Romans 10:12-15; 2 Timothy 4:1-5; 1 Peter 3:15; Revelation 20:15

When the Tag Was Changed

KEY VERSE

"'With man this is impossible, but with God all things are possible.'" Matthew 19:26

During the war, *triage* referred to the policy by which a decision was made as to what assistance would be given the wounded. It was up to the doctors to "color tag" the wounded, placing them in one of three categories according to the severity of their condition. Red stood for hopeless, nothing could be done to save them. Blue indicated that the only chance the person had was if medical assistance were given immediately. A yellow tag meant that the wounded soldier would make it even without treatment. Because medical supplies were limited, only those with blue tags received medical attention.

One day a soldier named Lou was brought in. He was severely wounded and one leg was badly blown apart. The doctor who examined him tagged him with a red tag, indicating that the case was hopeless, and left him to die. But a nurse noticed Lou was conscious and began to talk with him. After getting to know him as a person, she couldn't just let him die, so she broke the rules and replaced his red tag with a blue tag.

Lou was transported to the hospital in the back of a truck and spent the next several months there. Lou lived and the nurse he had met in the hospital became his wife. Although minus one leg, Lou was able to lead a full happy life because someone broke the rules and changed his tag.

APPLICATION

When you find yourself writing someone off as unreachable, remember that because of God's grace there is no such thing as an unreachable person.

ADDITIONAL SCRIPTURES

1 Samuel 16:7; Daniel 4:1-37; Jonah 1:1-3; 3:1-10; 4:1-11; Mark 5:1-20; 2 Peter 3:9

Our
Relationships
with
Others

Being a Witness
to Others

Wouldn't He Stick Out?

KEY VERSE

"And we, who with unveiled faces all reflect the Lord's glory, are being transformed into his likeness with ever-increasing glory, which comes from the Lord." 2 Corinthians 3:18

A seven-year-old boy approached his pastor one morning after the sermon. He said to the pastor, "Didn't you say I have to ask Jesus Christ into my heart in order to be a Christian?"

"That is what I said," replied the pastor.

"Well, how big is Jesus?" asked the boy.

"I'm not sure, but I bet He's pretty big, because He was a carpenter," the pastor told him.

"That's what I thought," said the little boy. "So as little as I am, and as big as Jesus is, wouldn't He stick out if I asked Him into my heart?"

To this the pastor smiled, "He will stick out more than you think."

APPLICATION

Being a Witness to Others

If Christ is in you there is no way to keep Him from "sticking out," because He will change your life from the inside out.

ADDITIONAL SCRIPTURES

Acts 9:1-22; Romans 12:1,2; 2 Corinthians 5:17; Galatians 2:20

Our
Relationships
with
Others

Being a Witness
to Others

Changing the Course of the River

"'Whoever welcomes a little child like this in my name welcomes me. But if anyone causes one of these little ones who believe in me to sin, it would be better for him to have a large millstone hung around his neck and to be drowned in the depths of the sea.'" Matthew 18:5,6

In Col. Heath Bottomly's book *The Prodigal Father* he tells the story of his father taking him and his brothers to Glacier Park in the Rockies. They climbed to the highest peak and stood, as it were, on the top of the world. They could see parts of four states and Canada.

As they looked over the edge, they could see the melting water split below. Some slid off to the west where it trickled from stream to lake and from river to river and finally reached the Pacific Ocean. A central tributary went straight ahead where, by way of the Yukon River, it found its way to the Arctic Ocean. And then one part slid off to the east where it finally ended up in the Mississippi River and then emptied into the Atlantic Ocean.

Then as his father led his brothers away, Heath lagged behind and made his way back to the rushing stream. He described the scene in his book:

I plunged my left hand into the rushing stream....It was ice cold. With all my strength I

pushed the stream over to the left. With my flat palm and wrist aching, I pressed the water over to the west and changed its course. I held it there though it fought and burned and ached. I gritted my teeth and pushed it hard.

Then his father arrived on the scene and carried him back to the trail. When they got back on the trail, his father squatted down and looked Heath in the eyes and said:

Son, I'm proud of you. You're nine years old and already trying to change the world. I watched you. That water was going into the Atlantic and you deliberately pushed it into the Pacific.

You have an opportunity to influence those around you, especially the children, either for good or for bad. Take that responsibility seriously.

Mark 9:42; Luke 17:1,2; Romans 14:13-19; 1 Corinthians 10:31-33

The Formerly Blind Leading the Blind

KEY VERSE

"Jesus said, 'For judgment I have come into this world, so that the blind will see and those who see will become blind.'" John 9:39

An eye surgeon, who went to China as a missionary, began practicing in one of China's hospitals. One of the first surgeries he performed was on a man who had been nearly blinded by cataracts. The operation was successful and the man recovered his eyesight.

A few weeks later, this missionary was greatly surprised when 48 blind men showed up on his hospital's doorstep. These blind men had walked more than 250 miles from a remote area of China to get to the hospital in order that they might have their sight restored. They had traveled the entire distance by holding on to a rope that kept them all together. And guess who had held the front end of the rope and led them all the way? It was the man who had his eyesight restored by the missionary surgeon!

Being a Witness
to Others

When you realize what God has done for us, you can't help but want to share that good news with other people.

Matthew 9:27-31; Luke 4:18; John 9:24-3, 35-41;
Acts 3:1-10; Romans 1:16; 10:13-15

- 208 -

Introduction

It is always amazing to me how a simple sentence or a quick statement can pull together a message and make it relevant. In fact there have been a few sermons I've heard where I wish the pastor would have summarized it with a short quote and sat down! I have found that the simple quote is often the entire "big idea" of a message. I carry pen and notebook with me at all times because you never know when that quote you have been looking for will enter your life.

Greg McKinnon has compiled some of my favorite quotes from the past and many new ones to use and adapt. Some of these quotes are so familiar that we don't even know who created them. Others are gems that we have discovered, tried and found to be effective. Of course we found others we tried that didn't work so we didn't put those in this book! We hope you'll enjoy and use these quotes to enhance your work with kids and their families.

Jim Burns, Ph.D.
President, National Institute of Youth Ministry
San Clemente, California

Christian Commitment

D. L. Moody once heard a preacher say, "The world has yet to see what God can do through one man completely committed to Him." That night D. L. Moody decided that he wanted to try to be that man.

God is not interested so much in our ability, as our availability.

The devil is willing for a person to confess Christianity as long as he does not practice it.

Jim Elliot was a young missionary who was killed by the Aouka Indians in Ecuador as he tried to share Christ with them. Before he died he wrote this in his journal one day: "He is no fool who gives that which he can not keep, in order to gain that which he cannot lose."

"Going to church doesn't make you a Christian any more than going to a garage makes you an automobile."
—Billy Sunday

Or the Southern version: "Sitting in church won't make you a Christian any more than sitting in the henhouse will make you a hen."

Forsaking
All
I
Take
Him.

Not to decide is to decide not.

God doesn't call us to be successful. He calls us to be faithful.

"Give me men who love nothing but God and hate nothing but sin."
—John Wesley

"Christ is not valued at all—unless He is valued above all."
—St. Augustine

"It doesn't take much of a man to be a Christian...it takes all of him."
—Dawson Trotman

It will cost you to be loyal to Christ, but it will cost you more not to be loyal.

Let's quit trying to use God and ask God to use us.

If God seems farther away, guess who moved.

Character

"Character is what you are in the dark."
—Dwight L. Moody

There is no right way to do the wrong thing.

If you don't stand for something, you will fall for anything.

"Right is always right, even if nobody is doing it and wrong is always wrong, even if everybody is doing it."
—Ben Haden

Maturity doesn't come with age; it comes with acceptance of responsibility.

Conscience…is that little voice that warns us somebody may be watching.

"Oh, yes," said the Indian, "I know what my conscience is. It is a little three-cornered thing in here," he laid his hand on his heart, "that stands still when I am good; but when I am bad it turns round, and the corners hurt very much. But if I keep on doing wrong, by-and-by the corners wear off and it doesn't hurt any more."
—J. Ellis

The fellow who is pulling the oars usually hasn't time to rock the boat.

It takes more courage to face grins than to face guns.

"Anger" is just one letter short of "danger."

Those who follow the crowd are quickly lost in it.

Our decisions must be based on what's right, not who is right.

People who tell white lies soon become color-blind.

Don't let your talk exceed your walk.

A wise man changes his mind; a fool never.

Reputation is what people think we are; character is what God knows we are.

If a man cannot be a Christian where he is, he cannot be a Christian anywhere.

Compromise is always wrong when it means a sacrifice of principles.

Don't worry when you stumble. Remember, a worm is about the only thing that can't fall down.

It is better to fail in doing right than to succeed in doing wrong.

God's work done in God's way will never lack God's supplies.

Habits are at first cobwebs, then cables.

The Bible has a word to describe "safe" sex: "marriage."

Anything worth doing is worth doing well.

Difficulty and Suffering

"Troubles are often the tools by which God fashions us for better things."
—Henry Ward Beecher

"Because of the cross, we are to bear one another's burdens and help carry one another's crosses, and when we do God turns our pain into joy."

—Toyhiko Kagawa, *Meditations on the Cross*

Smooth seas do not make skillful sailors.

I had no shoes, and I murmured, till I met a man who had no feet.

"God does not comfort us that we may be comfortable but that we may be comforters."
—Alexander Nowell

"If you are not failing now and again, it's a sign you're playing it safe."
—Woody Allen

We are all faced with a series of great opportunities brilliantly disguised as impossible situations.

"When testings come, we are purified; but when prosperity comes, we're vulnerable."
—Charles Swindoll

"Pray not for lighter burdens, but for stronger backs."
—Theodore Roosevelt

"Earth has no sorrow that Heaven cannot heal."
—Thomas Moore

"God never mends. He creates anew."
—Dwight L. Moody

When life kicks you, let it kick you forward.

God does not take away trials or carry us over them, but strengthens us through them.

A good way to forget your troubles is to help others out of theirs.

Evangelism

The only generation that can reach this generation is our generation.

Christianity is not a religion, it is a relationship.

"There is a hunger in the heart of man which none can satisfy, a vacuum which only God can fill."
— John Stott

Be careful how you live; you may be the only Bible that some people read.

Born once, die twice. Born twice, die once.

The world does not doubt Christianity as much as it does Christians.

Jesus Christ is not a crutch; He is the ground to walk on.

Some people think that God does not speak to men today, but He does! The trouble is that men refuse to listen.

People don't care how much you know until they know how much you care.

The Bible does not command sinners to go to church, but it does tell the church to go to sinners.

Generosity

"There is more power in the open hand than in the clenched fist."
— Herbert N. Cosson

We ought to learn to live more simply, so that others can simply live.

You can't outgive God.

"Money is not required to buy one necessity of the soul."
— Henry David Thoreau

"Make all you can, save all you can, give all you can."
— John Wesley

God's Attributes

"He loves each of us as if there were only one of us."
                              —Saint Augustine

Grace is God's riches at Christ's expense.

The cross is God's plus sign to a needy world.

If God were small enough to be understood, He would not be big enough to be worshiped.

Leadership

"To accomplish great things, we must not only act but also dream, not only plan but also believe."

—Anatole France

When a famous conductor was asked which instrument in the orchestra was the most difficult to play, he answered, "Second fiddle."

A man who wants to lead the orchestra must turn his back on the crowd.

The main thing is to keep the main thing the main thing.

"Even if you're on the right track, you're going to get run over if you sit there."

—Will Rogers

You can do anything if you don't care who gets the credit.

No pain, no gain!

The man who says, "It can't be done," is liable to be interrupted by someone doing it.

It is better to say, "This one thing I do," than "These forty things I dabble at."

Prayer

Praying will keep you from sinning, or sinning will keep you from praying.

"When we work, we work, when we pray, God works."
                    —Oswald Smith

"Do not pray for tasks equal to your powers. Pray for powers equal to your tasks."
                    —Phillips Brooks

If you are too busy to pray, you are too busy!

Prayer is not conquering God's reluctance, but taking hold of God's willingness.

Sin

"You're a fool, a simpleton, if you know what weakens you but feed on it anyway."
—Charles Swindoll

"Sin is not hurtful because it is forbidden, but it is forbidden because it is hurtful."
—Benjamin Franklin

The devil has no happy old men.

A person can pay now and play later, or he can play now and pay later.

A river becomes crooked by following the line of least resistance. So does a man!

Various Topics

THE BIBLE

The Bible does not need to be rewritten, but reread.

Men do not reject the Bible because it contradicts itself, but because it contradicts them.

HAPPINESS

Happiness is not happiness until it is given away.

FAITH

Faith is not twisting God's arm to give us what we want, but it's bending our will to do what God wants.

LEARNING

"I read and I forget, I see and I remember, I do and I understand."
— Confucius

LOVE

"Toil and zeal and even self-sacrifice are no substitute for love."
—Oswald Sanders in *Spiritual Maturity*

We too often love things and use people, when we should be using things and loving people.

A friend is someone who knows all about you and loves you just the same.

Contributors' Submissions

Wally Coats
Dunkirk

Mike DeVries
Breaking Out of Prison
The Pardon: A Louisiana Court Case
The Trial of Rudolf Hess

Joel Lusz
A Conference in Hell
After All He Has Done for Me
The Alcoholic Dad
Big Shot Lawyer
The Charlie Lubin Story
The Chicken and the Pig
The Class Address
Here Comes the Cat!
The "Sheep-Lion"

Dave Mahoney
A Lesson in Giving
A Lesson in Servanthood

Greg McKinnon
A Different Perspective
A Few Brownies Can Go a Long Way
A Riddle
A Strange Bird
Automatic Pilot
The Benefits of Suffering
Big Jim Took His Place
Broad Jumping the Grand Canyon
The Bumblebee
The Change Sin Can Bring
Change Your Name
Changing the Course of the River
Christ Knocking
Crowd Followers
Do It Now!
Do Unto Others As You Would Have Them Do Unto You
Forgetting the Basics
The Formerly Blind Leading the Blind
The Forty Martyrs of Sebaste
Give and It Will Be Given to You
God, Forgive Me When I Whine
God Goes Before Us
The Great Decision

How About a Nice Swim to Hawaii?
How to Catch a Monkey
"I Believe"
I'll Hold You Close
Is Anybody Else Up There?
Keeping Up Appearances
Keeping Up Your Guard
The Knitting Needle
Letter from a Communist
Making the Church Together
Martin and Morgan
Missed Opportunity
My Friend
Not Everyone Is Blind
Only the Applause of God
Paco
The Power of Our Words
Praying for God's Guidance
The Praying Hands
Prisoner of Sinful Desires
Recognized
The Right Choice
The Same Old Otis
Seven Days of Hooray and Whoop-Dee-Doo
She Knows Her Own
Some Things Are Immovable
Speaking the Language
Stained by the Blood
Strength for the Future
The Strength of One Testimony
Time Will Tell
Trying to Do the Job Alone
Trying to Stop Death
Twice God's
Wasted Away Due to Lack of Use
Watch Out for Those Tadpoles
We've Always Done It
When the Tag Was Changed
Who Changed the Price Tags?
Who Could Be More Important than the President?
Whose Duty Is It?
Wouldn't He Stick Out?
Yates Pool
You Tell Me
Your King
The Zode

Eddie Willis
Valentine's Day

Chuck Wysong
The "Bodies"
Changed Lives
Constitutional King or Prime Minister?
Free, But Still Locked Up
Good News
How to Make a Difference
I Am Grimaldi
I Knew You Would Come
Jesus Is in My Heart
Rescued
The Touch of the Master's Hand
Won't You Help Me?
You Can't Just Sit There

Scripture Reference Index
Old Testament

Page numbers in **boldface** type indicate Key Verses.

Page numbers in **boldface** type indicate Key Verses.

New Testament

Page numbers in **boldface** type indicate Key Verses.

Page numbers in **boldface** type indicate Key Verses.

Romans

1:1-11	124
1:16	208
2:24	194
3:22-24	50
3:22-26	54
3:22-28	56
3:23	**49**
4:2-8	54, 56
4:25	12
5:1-5	122, 186
5:3,4	**119**
5:3-5	120
5:6-8	12, 14, 150
5:8	**23**, 34, 50
5:8-10	30
5:17	62
6:2-18	132
6:4	86
6:14-18	92
6:16-18,22	26
6:23	28, **79**, 136
7:14-25	138
8:1,2	20, 26
8:9-11	78, 82
8:10	80
8:13	138
8:32	66
10:12-15	200
10:13,14	**187**
10:13-15	208
11:17-20	140
11:17-21	72
11:19-21	134
12:1,2	94, 102, 104, 204
12:2	**137**
12:3-8	178
12:4,5	174
12:4-8	160
12:10	164
12:19-21	184
13:8-10	168
13:14	52
14:12	**71**
14:13-19	206
14:19	170
15:1,2	154, 172
15:2	146

1 Corinthians

1:18-31	84
1:27, 28	44
1:27-29	172
2:9	**45**
2:9,10	29
2:14—3:3	92
3:1-3	100
3:10-15	128
6:20	16
9:19-22	191
9:22	**191**
9:24-27	96, 138
9:25	**139**
9:25-27	140
10:12	68, **129**
10:12,13	134
10:24,31-33	154
10:31	**125**
10:31-33	206
11:1	194
12:4-6	**159**
12:4-31	178
12:7-31	176
12:12,14-26	172
12:12-26	174
12:22,25	**171**
13:4,5	154
13:1-8	158
14:20	98
15:3,4	188
15:55-57	28
15:58	122

2 Corinthians

1:24	134
2:10,11	184
3:17	26
3:18	**203**
4:1	122
4:5	92, 191
4:8-18	106
4:18	116
5:7	**113**
5:9	128
5:14,15	**11**
5:17	**69, 85**, 204
5:20	**105**, 194

Page numbers in **boldface** type indicate Key Verses.

Page numbers in **boldface** type indicate Key Verses.

Page numbers in **boldface** type indicate Key Verses.

Page numbers in **boldface** type indicate Key Verses.

Topical Index

Add a New Member to Your Youth Staff.

Jim Burns is president of the National Institute of Youth Ministry.

Meet Jim Burns. He won't play guitar and he doesn't do windows, but he will take care of your programming needs. That's because his new curriculum, **YouthBuilders Group Bible Studies,** is a comprehensive program designed to take your group through their high school years. (If you have junior high kids in your group, **YouthBuilders** works for them too.)

For less than $6 a month, you'll get Jim Burns' special recipe of high-involvement, discussion-oriented, Bible-centered studies. It's the next generation of Bible curriculum for youth—and with Jim on your staff, you'll be free to spend more time one-on-one with the kids in your group.

Here are some of Youth-Builders' hottest features:

- Reproducible pages—one book fits your whole group
- Wide appeal—big groups, small groups—even adjusts to combine junior high/high school groups
- Hits home—special section to involve parents with every session of the study
- Interactive Bible discovery—geared to help young people find answers themselves
- Cheat sheets—a Bible *Tuck-In*™ with all the session information on a single page
- Flexible format—perfect for Sunday mornings, midweek youth meetings, or camps and retreats
- Three studies in one—each study has three four-session modules that examine critical life choices.

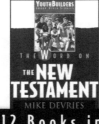

12 Books in the Series !

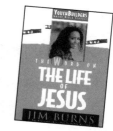

The Word on Sex, Drugs & Rock 'N' Roll
ISBN 08307.16424 $16.99

The Word on Prayer and the Devotional Life
ISBN 08307.16432 $16.99

The Word on the Basics of Christianity
ISBN 08307.16440 $16.99

The Word on Being a Leader, Serving Others & Sharing Your Faith
ISBN 08307.16459 $16.99

The Word on Helping Friends in Crisis
ISBN 08307.16467 $16.99

The Word on the Life of Jesus
ISBN 08307.16475 $16.99

The Word on Finding and Using Your Spiritual Gifts
ISBN 08307.17897 $16.99

The Word on the Sermon on the Mount
ISBN 08307.17234 $16.99

The Word on Spiritual Warfare
ISBN 08307.17242 $16.99

The Word on the New Testament
ISBN 08307.17250 $16.99

The Word on the Old Testament
ISBN 08307.17269 $16.99

The Word on Family
ISBN 08307.17277 $16.99

More Great Resources from Jim Burns

Drugproof Your Kids
Stephen Arterburn and Jim Burns

Solid biblical principles are combined with the most effective prevention and intervention techniques to give parents a guide they can trust.
ISBN 08307.17714 $10.99

Drugproof Your Kids Video
A 90-minute seminar featuring Stephen Arterburn and Jim Burns. Includes a reproducible syllabus.
SPCN 85116.00876 $19.99

Parenting Teens Positively
Video *Featuring Jim Burns*

Understand the forces shaping the world of a teenager and what you can do to be a positive influence. This powerful message of hope is for anyone working with—or living with—youth. Includes reproducible syllabus. UPC 607135.000655 $29.99

Surviving Adolescence
Jim Burns

Jim Burns helps teens—and their parents—negotiate the path from adolescence to adulthood with real-life stories that show how to make it through the teen years in one piece. ISBN 08307.20650 $9.99

For these and more great resources and to learn about NIYM's leadership training, call **1-800-397-9725.**

Gospel Light

FRESH IDEAS

RESOURCES FOR YOUTH WORKERS

Jim Burns, General Editor

Turn your youth group meetings into dynamic, exciting events that kids look forward to attending week after week! Supercharge your messages, grab their attention with your activities and connect with kids the first time and every time with these great resources. Just try to keep these books on the shelf!

ILLUSTRATIONS, STORIES AND QUOTES TO HANG YOUR MESSAGE ON
Few things get your point across faster or with greater impact than a memorable story with a twist. Grab your teens' attention by talking with your mouth full of unforgettable stories.
Manual, ISBN 08307.18834 **$16.99**

CASE STUDIES, TALK SHEETS AND DISCUSSION STARTERS
Teens learn best when they talk—not when you talk at them. A discussion allowing youth to discover the truth for themselves, with your guidance, is a powerful experience that will stay with them for a lifetime.
Manual, ISBN 08307.18842 **$16.99**

GAMES, CROWDBREAKERS AND COMMUNITY BUILDERS
Dozens of innovative, youth-group-tested ideas for fun and original crowdbreakers, as well as successful plans and trips for building a sense of community in your group.
Manual, ISBN 08307.18818 **$16.99**

More Resources for Youth Workers, Parents & Students

NATIONAL INSTITUTE OF YOUTH MINISTRY — NIYM

Steering Them Straight
Stephen Arterburn & Jim Burns

Parents can find understanding as well as practical tools to deal with crisis situations. Includes guidelines that will help any family prevent problems before they develop.
UPC 156179.4066 **$10.99**

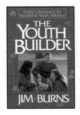

The Youth Builder
Jim Burns

This Gold Medallion Award winner provides you with proven methods, specific recommendations and hands-on examples of handling and understanding the problems and challenges of youth ministry.
ISBN 089081.1576. **$16.95**

Spirit Wings
Jim Burns

In the language of today's teens, these 84 short devotionals will encourage youth to build a stronger and more intimate relationship with God.
ISBN 08928.37837 **$10.95**

Radical Love
Book & Video, Jim Burns

In *Radical Love* kids discover why it's best to wait on God's timing, how to say no when their bodies say yes and how to find forgiveness for past mistakes.
Paperback, ISBN 08307.17935 **$9.99**
VHS Video, SPCN 85116.00922 **$19.99**

90 Days Through the New Testament
Jim Burns

A growth experience through the New Testament that lays the foundation for developing a daily time with God.
ISBN 08307.14561 **$9.99**

Getting in Touch with God
Jim Burns

Develop a consistent and disciplined time with God in the midst of hectic schedules as Jim Burns shares with you inspiring devotional readings to deepen your love of God.
ISBN 08908.15208 **$2.95**

Radical Christianity
Book & Video, Jim Burns

Radical Christianity is a proven plan to help youth live a life that's worth living and make a difference in their world.
Paperback, ISBN 08307.17927 **$9.99**
VHS Video, SPCN 85116.01082 **$19.99**

The Youth Worker's Book of Case Studies
Jim Burns

Fifty-two true stories with discussion questions to add interest to Bible studies.
ISBN 08307.15827 **$12.99**

To order NIYM resources, please call
1-800-397-9725
or to learn how you can take advantage of NIYM training opportunities call or write to:
NIYM • PO Box 297 • San Juan Capistrano
CA 92675 • 949/487-0217

What in the world is *NIYM*?

A.) The Neurotically Inclined Yo-Yo Masters
B.) The Neatest Incidental Yearbook Mystery
C.) The Natural Ignition Yields of Marshmallows
D.) The National Institute of Youth Ministry

If you deliberately picked A, B, or C you're the reason Jim Burns started NIYM! If you picked D, you can go to the next page. In any case, you could learn more about NIYM. Here are some IQ score-raisers:

Jim Burns started NIYM to:
• Meet the growing needs of training and equipping youth workers and parents
• Develop excellent resources and events for young people—in the U.S. and internationally
• Empower young people and their families to make wise decisions and experience a vital Christian lifestyle.

NIYM can make a difference in your life and enhance your youth work skills through these special events:

Institutes—These consist of week-long, in-depth small-group training sessions for youth workers.

Trainer of Trainees—NIYM will train you to train others. You can use this training with your volunteers, parents and denominational events. You can go through the certification process and become an official NIYM associate. (No, you don't get a badge or decoder ring).

International Training—Join NIYM associates to bring youth ministry to kids and adults around the world. (You'll learn meanings to universal words like "yo!" and "hey!')

Custom Training—These are special training events for denominational groups, churches, networks, colleges and seminaries.

Parent Forums—We'll come to your church or community with two incredible hours of learning, interaction and fellowship. It'll be fun finding out who makes your kids tick!

Youth Events—Dynamic speakers, interaction and drama bring a powerful message to kids through a fun and fast-paced day. Our youth events include: This Side Up, Radical Respect, Surviving Adolescence and Peer Leadership.

For brain food or a free information packet about the National Institute of Youth Ministry, write to:

NIYM
P.O. Box 297 • San Juan Capistrano, CA 92675
Tel: (949) 487-0217 • Fax: (949) 487-1758 • Info@niym.org